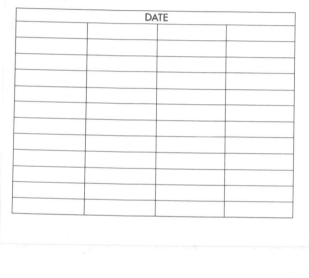

DATE			

AFRICAN SOCIETY TODAY

General editor: ROBIN COHEN

Advisory editors: O. Aribiah, Jean Copans,
Paul Lubeck, Philip M. Mbithi, M. S. Muntemba,
O. Nnoli, Richard Sandbrook

The series has been designed to provide scholarly, but lively and up-to-date, books, likely to appeal to a wide readership. The authors will be drawn from the field of development studies and all the social sciences, and will also have had experience of teaching and research in a number of African countries.

The books will deal with the various social groups and classes that comprise contemporary African society and successive volumes will link with previous volumes to create an integrated and comprehensive picture of the African social structure.

Also in the series

RURAL COMMUNITIES UNDER STRESS

Peasant farmers and the state in Africa

JONATHAN BARKER

Department of Political Science
University of Toronto

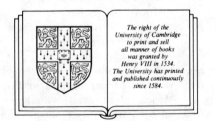

The right of the
University of Cambridge
to print and sell
all manner of books
was granted by
Henry VIII in 1534.
The University has printed
and published continuously
since 1584.

CAMBRIDGE UNIVERSITY PRESS

Cambridge

New York   Port Chester

Melbourne Sydney

Published by the Press Syndicate of the University of Cambridge
The Pitt Building, Trumpington Street, Cambridge CB2 1RP
40 West 20th Street, New York, NY 10011, USA
10 Stamford Road, Oakleigh, Melbourne 3166, Australia

First published 1989

Printed in Great Britain by Redwood Burn Limited, Trowbridge, Wiltshire

British Library cataloguing in publication data

Barker, Jonathan, 1938–
Rural communities under stress: peasant farmers and
the state in Africa. – (African society today).
1. Africa south of the Sahara. Rural communities.
Social conditions
1. Title. 11. Series
307.7′2′0967

Library of Congress cataloguing in publication data

Barker, Jonathan, 1938–
Rural communities under stress: peasant farmers and the state in
Africa/Jonathan Barker.
p.   cm. – (African society today)
Bibliography.
Includes index.
ISBN 0–521–30867–4. – ISBN 0–521–31358–9 (pbk.)
1. Agriculture and state – Africa, Sub-Saharan. 2. Farmers –
Government policy – Africa, Sub-Saharan. 3. Peasantry – Government
policy – Africa, Sub-Saharan. 4. Africa, Sub-Saharan – Rural
conditions. 1. Title. 11. Series
HD2120.S8B37 1989
338.1′86–dc19   89–519 CIP

ISBN 0 521 30867 4 hard covers
ISBN 0 521 31358 9 paperback

CONTENTS

ILLUSTRATIONS

FIGURES

MAPS

TABLES

ACKNOWLEDGMENTS

The ideas which find expression here were nourished by the help of many friends and strangers over many years. My parents Roger Barker and Louise Barker showed me how a person can think clearly and care deeply at the same time. The Social Science and Humanities Research Council of Canada gave me support for several stints of field research which I draw upon in these pages. The research trips brought me the chance to learn from the people of Birkelane, Senegal and Vwawa, Tanzania and from people who live and work in villages and agricultural projects in Sudan, Mozambique, and Côte d'Ivoire. I draw freely on their teachings in this book.

Friends and colleagues in Toronto, Dar es Salaam, Khartoum, Abidjan, Dakar, Maputo, Sussex, and Los Angeles shared ideas and gave encouragement. Several generations of students in the course on rural change in Africa at the University of Toronto brought me ideas and information and helped me to improve my analysis of many important issues. Robin Cohen, the series editor, gave good advice and strong support. Nicholas Thompson, Penny Thompson, Gillian Barker, Susan van de Ven, Hugh Dow and Anne Bryden improved the writing.

Behind this short book is a long journey shared most intimately by Nancy Sears Barker. She gets special thanks.

§ 1 §

DRAMAS OF RURAL CHANGE

Disaster in rural sub-Saharan Africa has become a regular, almost annual event in recent years.[1] In 1985 it was estimated that 10 million Africans left their homes and fields because they were unable to support themselves and that an additional 20 million were reported to be at risk of debilitating hunger. More than twenty countries had significant numbers of citizens at risk. Drought was the immediate cause of this widespread disaster, as it had been in the Sahel region just south of the Sahara desert in the mid 1970s when the first great postwar relief effort for Africa was mobilized. Drought, along with civil strife, also played a part in the famines in Ethiopia in 1984 and 1988 (Timberlake 1985).

In 1987 and 1988 millions in Mozambique were in peril of starvation, but drought was only a minor cause; the major reason for the catastrophic failure in food production was the war of economic destruction conducted by the government of South Africa. The consequences, however, were similar to those of drought, as thousands, perhaps millions, of peasant farmers set out walking in search of a way to survive (*The Toronto Star*, 15 March 1987). It is certain that more such calamities will occur in

This study encompasses Africa south of the Sahara, with the exception of South Africa.

Table 1 *Sub-Saharan Africa: basic statistics*

Country or region	Population (millions)	GNP per capita ($, 1986)	Growth of GNP per capita (1965–86, average %)	Urban population (% of 1985 total)	Years life expectancy (1986)
All low-income countries	2493.0	270	3.1	22	61
Sub-Saharan Africa	424.1	370	0.9	25	50
Angola	9.0	NA	NA	25	44
Benin	4.2	270	0.2	35	50
Botswana	1.1	840	8.8	20	59
Burkina Faso[a]	1.3	150	1.3	8	47
Burundi	4.8	240	1.8	2	48
Cameroon	10.5	910	3.9	42	56
Central African Republic	2.7	290	−0.6	45	50
Chad	5.1	NA	NA	27	45
Congo	2.0	990	3.6	40	58
Côte d'Ivoire	10.7	730	1.2	45	52
Ethiopia	43.5	120	0	15	46
Gabon	1.0	3080	1.9	12	52
Ghana	13.2	390	−1.7	32	54
Guinea	6.3	NA	NA	22	42
Kenya	21.2	300	1.9	20	57
Lesotho	1.6	370	5.6	17	55
Liberia	2.3	460	−1.4	37	54
Malawi	7.4	160	1.5	NA	45
Mali	7.6	180	1.1	20	47
Mauritania	1.8	420	−0.3	31	47
Mozambique	14.2	210	NA	19	48
Niger	6.6	260	−2.2	15	44
Nigeria	103.1	640	1.9	30	51
Rwanda	6.2	290	1.5	5	48
Senegal	6.8	420	−0.6	36	47
Sierra Leone	3.8	310	0.2	25	41
Somalia	5.5	280	−0.3	34	47
Sudan	22.6	320	−0.2	21	49
Tanzania	23.0	250	−0.3	14	53
Togo	3.1	250	0.2	23	53
Uganda	15.2	230	−2.6	7	48
Zaire	31.7	160	−2.2	39	52
Zambia	6.9	300	−1.7	46	53
Zimbabwe	8.7	620	1.2	27	58

Note: Tables 1, 2, 4 and 5 include data on the countries of sub-Saharan Africa with populations of 1 million and over (excepting South Africa).
[a] Burkina Faso was formerly known as Haute Volta.

Source: World Bank 1988, pp. 222 and 284.

Africa, most likely in those large regions where unreliable rainfall makes agriculture risky, where environmental damage is increasing in severity and where civil disorder may interrupt the cycle of cultivation. The address of the next victims is not known, but we who watch television will once again see pictures of thousands of uprooted people straggling across uncultivated landscapes and gathered in temporary settlements, sometimes receiving handouts sufficient to keep them alive.

The starving and displaced are the most publicized and heart-wrenching manifestation of a profound and many-sided endeavour by millions of Africans to maintain and improve their livelihoods on the land. Their resilience and initiative are only rarely captured in television pictures, but occasionally we are shown refugees leaving the camps where international assistance has kept them alive. The rains returned or peace restored, we see the survivors setting out on the march back to their lands of origin intending to rebuild their communities and economies. They organize themselves once again to employ their skills as farmers and use their social knowledge to recreate a way of life. Even where there has been no catastrophe, the effort to adjust, to build, and to rebuild ways of farming and living in a community is a continuing preoccupation. Catastrophes are recognized as such when almost everybody in a region is rendered helpless. Much more common is a situation far short of a general disaster where 10 to 30 per cent of the population is afflicted by hunger, but where few are helpless. Richer and poorer are doing what they have the means to do and what they can think of doing to survive and prosper.

There are happier dramas as well: the statistics on the rapid spread of schooling in Africa (secondary school enrollments was up over the period 1965–1984 from 6 per cent of the age group to 27 per cent) and rising life expectancy (up by about 7 years in the period 1965–1985) are outward measures of teacher-training drives, public health measures, and construction programmes, many of which are pushed and promoted by the communities they benefit (World Bank 1987, 259, 263). In some regions many farming groups have successfully adopted new crops or improved techniques of cultivation, thereby achieving growing economic prosperity. Agricultural research in Africa is finally gaining some systematic knowledge of how to improve the quantity and reliability of the production of such basic foods as cassava, cowpeas, millet, and sorghum. Realistic methods of improving the fertility and moisture retention of poor and rain-starved soils are gaining acceptance (Harrison 1987).

More controversial are the dozens of huge development schemes damming and diverting rivers to generate electricity and irrigate farmland. Governments and funding agencies are all too easily convinced that they can put farming on a reliable and productive footing, but very few large schemes have succeeded. Aside from huge technical problems, they run up against social reality. They disorganize and incapacitate whole communities by resettling them and demanding that they learn entirely new ways of farming. Spontaneous population movement can also disrupt agriculture. When young people leave farming communities they may succeed in finding work in a city or in a more prosperous farming area which improves their economic prospects. Yet their departure deprives the home community of labour, talent, and ambition.

The dramas are not all economic and demographic; they also involve the rise of new local leaders, both cultural and political. Religious creativity is continually responding to new moral dilemmas faced by rural people under the pressure of changing family relations, the threat of impoverishment and the choices of new wealth. Governments and political movements also play a central role in rural change. They strengthen or weaken rural voices and enhance or harm the infrastructure and pricing regime of the farming system. Governments and political movements also respond – negatively or positively – to the cultural claims of agricultural communities.

The purpose of this book is to look beneath the large disasters and beyond the efforts of individuals, families and communities to the deeper logics in peasant farming in sub-Saharan Africa. The 'logics' are plural because the situations of peasant farming communities are various. The task of the book is to introduce the forces at work in peasant farming and to show how different combinations of endeavour and circumstance shape the experience and prospects of the rural population.

RURAL AFRICA UNDER PRESSURE

By far the majority of the population of tropical Africa lives in rural areas. While the urban population is growing especially rapidly, the rural population is also increasing at unprecedented rates. In mid 1985 the population of sub-Saharan Africa was 418 million and forecast to reach 500 million in the early 1990s. In 1980 settlements classified as rural were home to 75 per cent of the population. In the late 1980s, about 350 million sub-Saharan Africans live in rural areas and constitute more than 70 per cent of the total population (World Bank 1987, 205, 257, 267).

Although there are many different rural occupations (including crafts, commerce, services, and government), the large majority of rural dwellers works in agriculture. Some of those working in agriculture have other occupations as well, such as carpentry or retail trade. The figures on employment in major economic sectors confirm the importance of agriculture (Table 2). In 1980 fully 75 per

Table 2 Sub-Saharan Africa: importance of agriculture

Country or region	% of labour force in agriculture (1980)	% of labour force in agriculture (1965)	% of GDP in agriculture (1986)	% of GDP in agriculture (1965)
All low-income countries	72	77	32	42
Sub-Saharan Africa	75	79	36	45
Burundi	93	94	58	NA
Rwanda	93	94	40	75
Niger	91	95	46	68
Burkina Faso	87	89	45	53
Mali	86	90	50	NA
Uganda	86	91	76	52
Tanzania	86	92	59	46
Lesotho	86	92	21	65
Mozambique	85	87	35	NA
Malawi	83	92	37	50
Chad	83	92	NA	42
Kenya	81	86	30	35
Senegal	81	83	22	25
Guinea	81	87	40	NA
Ethiopia	80	86	48	58
Somalia	76	81	58	71
Gabon	75	83	10	26
Liberia	74	79	37	27
Togo	73	78	32	45
Zambia	73	79	11	14
Zimbabwe	73	79	11	18
Zaire	72	82	29	21
Central African Republic	72	88	41	46
Sudan	71	82	35	54
Benin	70	83	49	59
Sierra Leone	70	78	45	34
Botswana	70	89	4	34
Cameroon	70	86	22	32
Mauritania	69	89	34	32
Nigeria	68	72	41	53
Côte d'Ivoire	65	81	36	47
Congo	62	66	8	19
Ghana	56	61	45	44
Angola	56	69	NA	NA

Source: World Bank 1988, pp. 226 and 282.

cent of the region's economically active people worked in agriculture. The proportion had dropped only four percentage points from 79 per cent in 1965 (World Bank 1987, 265).

The importance of the rural sector is measured not only in terms of the proportion of the population living and working in rural areas. Agriculture forms the core economy for most of sub-Saharan Africa. For the region as a whole agriculture accounted for 36 per cent of gross domestic product (GDP) in 1986, down from 45 per cent in 1965. Services – including government, trade and transport – ranked higher, at 37 per cent of GDP in 1985, but many of them are closely linked to agricultural exports (World Bank 1988, 227). There are very important variations, as will be shown below, but for most countries individual livelihoods and government revenue are overwhelmingly dependent on agriculture (Table 2). Although there are places where many rural people work for wages, it remains true that rural people usually grow most of the food eaten in rural communities and that they earn cash by growing crops for sale in international and national markets. This is not to say that they are self-sufficient; their purchases may be essential for their needs as consumers and as producers. At the same time, self-provisioning remains crucial to their survival and well-being.

Agriculture is also important for other sectors of the economy. Trade and services in rural towns are closely linked to agricultural production and sales. Government revenue comes from taxes or levies on agricultural exports, often only one, two, or three major crops, each the product of a region specializing in that crop. Even the countries where export earnings and government revenue come mainly from mineral exports (Nigeria, Zambia, Zaire, Angola, Botswana, Gabon, Congo), there is usually a large rural population dependent on healthy agriculture.

For all countries, but especially those with higher incomes, growing sufficient food to meet current demand means an important gain in foreign exchange. A large proportion of the staple grains (wheat and rice) for many of Africa's urban dwellers is now imported (Huddleston 1984; Mellor, Delgado, and Blackie 1987).

Rural Africa is on the move (Stichter 1985). Some of the movement is cyclical, like the regular migration of transhumant pastoralists who graze the driest areas during the short season of rains and then move to wetter areas to take advantage of the stubble left in the fields after harvest and the grass which grows in and near harvested fields. People in regions with no cash crop or with a long dead season go for seasonal work in other places, sometimes across national boundaries. Peasant farmers from the Sahel zone have long spent some months of each year as agricultural workers or tenant farmers (often paying in labour for the use of land) in the more intensive cash crop zones near the coast. The rural regions of Lesotho and southern Mozambique have sent hundreds of thousands of men to the mines of South Africa on 12- to 24-month contracts. Some men return repeatedly on new contracts; others go only once or twice. There is also a population flow to and from the towns and cities, following the rhythm of agricultural work and responding to the agricultural fortunes of families or regions.

Other movements and changes in population are not cyclical, but represent a flow of change in a definite direction. One of the most powerful changes with the broadest implications is the rise of the rural population (Table 3). On the average in tropical Africa, the rural population is growing at the rate of about 3 per cent each year. At that rate the rural population will double in twenty-three years, although, of course, the rates vary greatly from place to place. The rapid population growth reflects advances in health and sanitation which have reduced the mortality rate of infants and young children. Experience elsewhere indicates that an increasing material standard of living is a powerful influence decreasing the number of children people desire. Africa's high rate of population growth is as much a result as it is a cause of poor economic performance. But even at that average rate, such growth cannot be absorbed simply by reproducing and extending the same family, community, and productive structures. Historically in rural Africa a common response to social and economic pressures of the kind brought on by population growth has been to split a family, a village, or a community in two, letting each part form a new whole going its own way. Now, however, more profound changes are well under way.

The large number of infants and children raises the ratio of dependants to working adults, increases the demands of child care and education, and forces peasant farmers to cultivate land more intensively and to bring less productive, more distant, and generally less desirable land under cultivation. The steady net flow of people from villages and farms to cities is fed by those who have found it impossible to earn an acceptable living in the countryside. If urban economies were growing rapidly and creating new jobs, cityward migration would be a measure of growing productivity. Unfortunately in Africa the positive forms of urban migration are overshadowed by the negative ones. The huge movement of people from drought-stricken areas to cities is only the most dramatic manifestation of a much more widespread dynamic. The pressure on rural communities pushes marginal farmers who have no prospect of earning a living in farming and school leavers with some hope of finding urban wage work into the stream of rural people bound for the cities. Even in Zambia, where the work and the wealth in copper mining created a boom in urban employment in the 1960s, and in Nigeria, where oil revenues financed a huge construction spree in the 1970s, the precipitous decline in export prices abruptly reduced the demand for labour. The pressure of inadequate rural livelihood is not relieved by possibilities for urban employment, since the urban sector faces an employment crisis of its own. The paradoxical political implications of the linked rural and urban crises are discussed further in chapter 8.

There are many other indicators of pressures on rural society. On the average in rural Africa the shortfall in the meeting of basic needs has grown in the past twenty-five years. The pressures on rural Africa are measured on a continental scale by statistics showing that agriculture is growing more slowly than population (Table 3). Food production in sub-Saharan Africa in recent years has dropped increasingly below demand; imports of basic food grains rose to almost 4 million metric tons of cereals in 1974 and close to 9 million in 1986 (Table 4). Imports in that year accounted for about one-fifth of the cereals consumed by the 424 million people in the region. The pressures on rural society and the shortfalls in agricultural production are unevenly distributed, as the data by country reveal (Table 5). The statistical data are not firm enough to sustain a clear conclusion about the location and circumstances of food supply shortages in rural Africa, but there is little doubt that the problem is widespread.

The immediate experience of crisis for many rural people is a lack of opportunity to work productively. One of the most disquieting statistics shows a decrease in the average productivity of each rural worker. This means that for the region as a whole a combination of ecological degradation, maldistribution of land, civil disturbance, poor market incentives, and inadequate supply of inputs

Table 4 *Sub-Saharan Africa: self-sufficiency in agriculture*

Country or region	Cereal imports			Food aid in cereals		Average index[a] of food production per capita
	kilos per capita 1986	thousands of metric tons 1986	thousands of metric tons 1974	thousands of metric tons 1985/86	thousands of metric tons 1974/75	1984–86
All low-income countries	7	18 038	21 897	6384	5710	114
Sub-Saharan Africa	21	8730	3931	3655	910	97
Malawi	1	6	17	5	0	90
Uganda	1	17	37	7	0	111
Burundi	3	14	7	6	6	98
Rwanda	4	24	3	25	19	87
Zimbabwe	6	54	56	NA	0	92
Niger	7	43	155	97	73	85
Kenya	9	189	15	139	2	87
Tanzania	11	244	431	66	148	92
Zaire	11	361	343	101	1	100
Ghana	12	154	177	96	33	109
Benin	13	55	8	11	9	114
Cameroon	14	149	81	12	4	94

Country					
Central African Republic	15	40	7	11	1	94
Nigeria	15	1596	389	0	7	103
Chad	16	83	37	74	20	100
Togo	21	66	6	9	11	91
Zambia	21	148	93	82	5	96
Mali	24	181	281	83	107	101
Guinea	24	151	63	55	49	93
Ethiopia	24	1047	118	793	54	87
Mozambique	28	393	62	252	34	85
Sudan	28	636	125	904	46	96
Angola	31	276	49	53	0	90
Sierra Leone	34	130	72	49	10	97
Somalia	50	274	42	126	111	98
Congo	52	104	34	2	2	93
Liberia	54	124	42	76	3	99
Côte d'Ivoire	56	601	172	0	4	105
Burkina Faso	63	82	99	109	28	112
Gabon	74	74	13	NA	NA	98
Senegal	80	544	341	117	27	102
Lesotho	90	144	49	40	14	82
Mauritania	116	209	115	137	48	88
Botswana	128	141	21	49	5	76

Note: [a] 1979–81 = 100.

Source: World Bank 1988, pp. 222 and 234.

Table 5 *Sub-Saharan Africa: change in agriculture*

Country or region	Percent of annual growth in agricultural production		Fertilizer consumption in hundreds of grams per hectare of arable land	
	1980–86	1965–80	1985	1970
All low income countries	4.9	2.7	674	168
Sub-Saharan Africa	1.2	1.6	91	32
Somalia	7.9	NA	36	31
Zimbabwe	3.4	NA	622	466
Benin	3.0	NA	66	33
Niger	2.8	−3.4	10	1
Kenya	2.8	4.9	460	224
Zambia	2.8	2.2	155	71
Burkina Faso	2.7	NA	46	3
Malawi	2.5	NA	143	52
Central African Republic	2.5	2.1	15	11
Senegal	2.3	1.4	55	20
Cameroon	2.0	4.2	81	28
Zaire	1.7	NA	10	8
Togo	1.7	1.9	69	3
Lesotho	1.6	NA	117	17
Nigeria	1.4	1.7	108	3
Burundi	1.3	3.3	18	5
Mauritania	1.2	−2.0	103	6
Liberia	1.2	5.5	100	55
Rwanda	0.9	NA	14	3
Côte d'Ivoire	0.9	3.3	118	71
Tanzania	0.8	1.6	76	30
Sierra Leone	0.5	2.3	20	13
Sudan	0.4	2.9	75	31
Guinea	0.3	NA	2	18
Uganda	−0.1	1.2	0	13

Table 5 *(cont.)*

Country or region	Percent of annual growth in agricultural production		Fertilizer consumption in hundreds of grams per hectare of arable land	
	1980–86	1965–80	1985	1970
Ghana	−0.2	1.6	44	9
Congo	−0.6	3.1	69	112
Mali	−2.3	2.8	129	29
Ethiopia	−3.9	1.2	47	4
Botswana	−9.8	9.7	4	14
Mozambique	−15.9	NA	12	27
Chad	NA	NA	23	7
Gabon	NA	NA	62	0
Angola	NA	NA	58	45

Source: World Bank 1988, pp. 224 and 234.

(such as hoes, machetes, selected seed, and fertilizer) is forcing an economic decline (World Bank 1981).

To the difficulties of production, ecological balance, and social integrity must now be added the pandemic of the acquired immune deficiency syndrome (AIDS) which threatens to incapacitate and eventually kill a very large number of people around the world. The disease appears to be well established in many African countries, particularly in urban centres of East and Central Africa, and its spread to many parts of rural Africa can be anticipated. The population projections cited above may have to be reduced to take account of the rising mortality of children born with the disease and the increased death rate among women of childbearing age. This manner of dampening

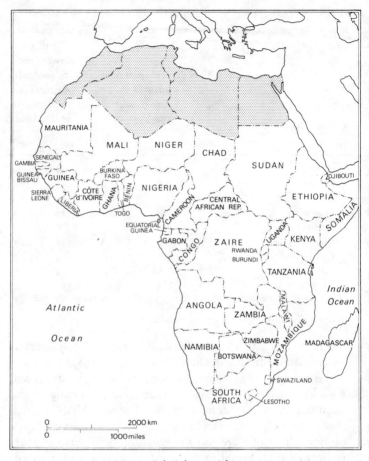

Map 1 Sub-Saharan Africa

population growth will not ease the pressure on social labour. By rendering some proportion of the able and productive members of communities unproductive and dependent, by overwhelming care-giving resources, and by contributing to a sense of moral distress, the disease will add very substantially to the burden of rural (and urban) communities and government institutions (*New Scientist* 17 March 1988, 30–31).

There are other changes which are neither cyclical nor unidirectional. On the whole the cultivation of export and cash crops for sale on the internal market have grown since the imposition of colonial rule. For most of the period from 1900 to 1929 the terms of trade for African export crops were favourable, and this encouraged peasant farmers in many countries to begin producing for the world market on a large scale. The depression years and the unfavourable trend in trade from 1930 to 1945 focussed economic pressures on all those who had invested in export production. Administrative pressures and the need to maintain a cash income forced peasant farmers to produce and even to expand production. Then in the decade after World War Two there was a sharp rise in the relative price of exports and a great spurt of growth in export production, carrying on into the 1960s (Levi and Havinden 1982, 32–33). In many areas it has continued, sometimes at a slower pace. However, in the past two decades export production in some regions has suffered a decline.

Global statistics only hint at such changes and provide even less insight into the overall impact of equally important changes in basic aspects of rural society: rural settlement patterns, distribution of control of land and other wealth, availability of school places and health services, farming practices, and geographical movement of labour. In one sense the dearth of global statistics is not as grave a gap as might appear: in themselves quantitative measures of change have little global meaning. Their meaning comes from the specific structural context to which they belong. One of the contentions of this book is that rural change is best understood when it is situated in its proper national and local context.

Rhythms of change

Even without resort to statistics, evidence of the pace and depth of change in Africa is visible in the rural social landscape. Imagine a speeded-up film depicting change in the constructed environment of rural Africa in the past eighty years. On the first reel seaports appear and expand, rail lines and roads penetrate from the port cities toward enlarging mines and spreading fields of cotton, peanuts (groundnuts), and cocoa. In Ghana the rows of long narrow cocoa farms extending back into the forest from a path or roadway make a striking pattern. Large farms with rectilinear fields are carved out in the highlands of Kenya and the fertile parts of the Rhodesian plateau, while a few large rubber and oil palm plantations expand in Liberia and the Belgian Congo, and sisal estates appear in Tanganyika. In Sudan above the confluence of the Niles a rare feature appears: a large irrigated farming zone.

In the new cash-crop zones along the roads and railroads the typical squares of official markets are thrust into view bringing new towns or reformed villages around them. The housing of the merchant and official class is easy to distinguish from the houses of the ordinary townspeople. With the great depression of the 1930s there is a pause in large-scale construction. Cash crop zones, on the other hand, continue to spread out from their core areas. New land is cleared for farming in the forest zones, and in the more open country fields invade the areas formerly used solely by moving pastoralists.

With the end of World War Two there is a great surge of change in the human landscape. The cash-crop areas expand rapidly and some new ones are formed: coffee farms managed by Portuguese immigrants replace peasant agriculture in north-central Angola; peanuts and cotton spread into Mali, Niger, Haute Volta, and Chad; tea, coffee, and pyrethrum spread in East Africa. Coffee and cocoa claim a large part of the forest zone of Côte d'Ivoire. The equatorial forests themselves shrink rapidly as they are logged and the timber exported.

The growth of the rural population is apparent in the expanding size and number of villages. Cities spread, and around the larger ones vast peri-urban zones which are neither urban nor rural come into existence. Road networks push further and the main roads are widened and surfaced. Schools, post offices, police posts, and health centres rise near the administrative and military posts in rural towns and in some of the larger villages as administrative buildings are extended into smaller administrative divisions. Mosques and churches become more numerous.

There is little on the film of the social landscape to mark the passage to independence. A close observer may notice that new schools and administrative buildings appear at an even faster rate, road construction continues apace, and new neighbourhoods of middle-class housing rise swiftly in cities and towns. By 1970 the pace of major new construction falls and by 1980 it is confined to a few countries. In others, notably Zaire and Uganda, there is striking disintegration as roads fall into disuse and buildings are left to decay. Still, the smaller construction of village homes continues, new land is brought under the hoe, and forest and savanna continue to fall to cultivation.

Regional patterns

On return from a recent visit to agricultural settings in five countries of sub-Saharan Africa, I eagerly studied the photographs I had taken only to discover that almost all of them recorded a vast landscape and an enormous sky bisected by a wide horizon. Most of rural Africa is open grassland, savanna with scattered trees, or broad river valleys. Where rainfall is higher and occurs through most of the year, the forest is more dense. The substantial differences between savanna and forest agriculture are described in chapter 4. Yet not all of rural Africa is flat. The rift valley, the volcanic mountains of East Africa and Cameroon, and smaller upland regions elsewhere contain important areas of steeply sloped fields and narrow watered valleys.

These climatic and geomorphological differences impress themselves on agricultural practices in the different regions of the continent. However, it is interesting to note that it is not possible to account for differences in agricultural population density in terms of soil fertility or annual rainfall. Among the most heavily occupied areas are the appropriately named 'Closely Settled Zone' around Kano, Nigeria and the highland states of Rwanda and Burundi. In all three cases geopolitical forces seem to have determined the extraordinary densities and unusually intensive farming practices. Geography alone does not create the important regional differences which characterise peasant farming in Africa (and which receive further examination in chapter 4).

Such is the large pattern of rural change in Africa. It is driven by the expansion of markets, the increasing ease of transportation, and the rise in population. Some of its core elements (as explained in chapter 5) are organized from above by governments (both colonial and post-colonial), by transnational business organizations, and by international aid agencies. The changing spatial organization of rural communities is evidence of changes in the distribution of political power and in social influence. Hidden within the population movements, the raising of houses, the leveling of forests, and the concentration of village settlements are myriad social dramas of conflicting values, troubled consciences, and clashing wills (a topic elaborated in chapter 6). Along with the creation of a new market town comes the construction of a new base of social and political power, or the reshaping of an old one. Along with the spreading network of retail trade and purchase points for export crops comes a chain of jobs and of favours given or refused, which in many cases forms part of a ramifying system of political patronage and economic accumulation (a matter which is discussed at length in chapters 7 and 8).

Smaller dramas

In farming families (the subject of chapter 3) there is often a degree of tension about the attempts of heads of families to control the labour of the group, usually the wives and young adult children. Where a woman is the head of the household (especially common where men go elsewhere to work), the issue of authority in the household raises the question of the proper role of women especially sharply. The opportunity and often the necessity for cash income from agriculture may raise the stakes and engage issues about the proper authority of parents and husbands, the value of cash income as opposed to food crops, and the claims of youth for cultural and economic freedom. These issues may never reach any formally public or political arena, yet for the family and community they may be very important political issues. Another source of frequent contention in rural Africa is change over the way in which use of land is inherited, exchanged, and acquired. Such issues (which are studied more deeply in chapter 6) may appear only in discussions or tensions within local communities or even within kin groups, but at that level they are significant political issues.

There are the many smaller dramas of families faced

with poor harvests deciding whether to migrate to little-known regions, of governments faced with falling revenues deciding whether or not to raise taxes on agricultural products, of women deciding to demand a fairer share of family cash income in recompense for work on cash crops, of villagers uniting to build a well or a school and to demand that government reward their efforts with a pump or a teacher, or of villagers displaced by drought deciding to return to their homes on learning that rains have returned. Some of the small dramas are happy ones: Ghanaian villages rediscovering crafts neglected in recent years, revaluing the art of subsistence agriculture complemented by harvesting wild game and wild plants; women banding together to grow food in an insurance field, the harvest of which will be used by the most needy families; young families moving into frontier zones to clear and plant new lands; and small irrigation projects working well through good local organization and judicious help from external agencies.

In the board rooms, government offices, and hotel suites where International Monetary Fund (IMF) representatives, international bankers, and World Bank officials meet with one another and with government representatives, other dramas are staged. Their scripts revolve around the power of money: loans, credit performance standards, and project definition. In settings culturally and physically far removed from the homesteads, fields and pastures of the rural producers, decisions are taken with wide effect on production and transport costs to farmers, on the prices they receive for their crops and on the kinds of organizations with which they must deal.

Farming people are not entirely helpless in the face of decisions made for them. In many countries and on a number of occasions they have expressed their displeasure at the ballot box. Often they can give careful and polite voice to their complaints by speaking to local officials, representatives, or political patrons. In a few instances they have turned to open resistance and protest as in the *Agbekoya* rebellion in the cocoa area of western Nigeria in 1968–69 (Beer and Williams 1974) and in the *Sungusungu* movement in the western cotton zone of Tanzania in the late 1970s (Mapolu 1986, 129). More frequently they contrive ways to circumvent regulations and organizations which work against their interests. Sometimes they can create or sustain alternative marketing channels (variously called unofficial, parallel, black, informal, or clandestine) which avoid government prices, taxes, and regulations to sell on local markets or across national borders. These forms of political action are the topic of chapter eight.

The dramas are not only political and economic in their content. Pressures on family and community authority raise moral and religious issues which may divide men and women, elders and youth, and religious group from religious group. The dramas also have wider implications for the economies and governments of sub-Saharan Africa.

TRENDS AND ISSUES

That rapid and definitive change is under way in rural Africa is not in doubt; what is in doubt is its speed, the pain and destruction it brings, and the qualities of the society to which it gives rise. Not all the signs are negative. Nine African countries in 1980–86 kept agricultural production above or close to population growth levels and at least four countries improved their production over the previous fifteen years (Table 4). Agricultural research is finally showing positive results for crops and methods which might actually fit the needs, schedules, and capacities of peasant farmers. Governments and international economic agencies are placing unprecedented emphasis on rural development. However, the long record of poor production, the vulnerability of large regions to poor rains, the weaknesses of the research programs, the low world prices for agricultural products, and the weaknesses in many places of the transportation and administration infrastructures all make it seem likely that an endemic agricultural crisis will continue in much of sub-Saharan Africa. That particular regions and countries will suffer catastrophic disasters in the wake of droughts and wars is certain.

Because of the central role of the agricultural economy, its poor performance has broad implications throughout the society. Peasant farmers unable to produce adequately leave the land and make their way to the cities, fueling an unprecedented rate of urbanization which is creating enormous problems of employment, housing, and sanitation in the cities. Similar population movements within rural areas pour new demands for land and work into areas less affected by drought or poor producer prices. Occupations that may appear very distant from farming are directly hit by production shortfalls. Rural trade is sapped by the drop in demand. Import–export trade is similarly constricted. Trucking and transport lose business directly, as fewer crops need to be moved, and indirectly, as farmers and traders with lower incomes and less business make fewer calls for trucking or rail services. Spending on weddings, funerals, and religious celebrations also declines and the merchants and service-sector workers who cater to these activities are pinched.

Governments plagued by revenue shortages and balance-of-payment deficits become weakened and lose control over policy decisions. They also cut back their contracts for construction and services. They may even have trouble paying salaries and therefore move to orderly or chaotic contraction of their roster of employees. Thus the political consequences of the conditions of the rural economy are palpable, but they go much deeper and much wider than their effects on government revenue.

Economic failure can trigger a crisis in values and culture and lead to new social movements. The mechanisms may be complex, as competing theories about religious change in rural Africa suggest, but the existence of cultural tensions in rural Africa is widely accepted (this will be explored later in some case studies). Something that distinguishes peasant farming is the fact that production relations are also very often family relations. New forms of production management mean new relations between husbands and wives and adults and children. Change in production therefore engages very directly a whole set of basic cultural values about family, education, gender relations, and moral behaviour generally in family and community. It is only logical that economic change and changes in values and meaning should go hand in hand under these conditions. Some revealing examples will be discussed in chapter 8.

A question of special interest for this book has to do with the relations between community politics and state politics. Although their emphases may conflict, many scholars argue that state and community politics work at cross purposes. One view is that the issues and groups which stir up community politics have a destructive impact as they penetrate and influence state politics. Ethnic issues and kinship loyalties motivate special favours and corrupt practices which destroy administrative rationality and undercut economic efficiency. State decisions about allocation of activity and investment are thrown into disarray by the necessity to satisfy community claims.

Another view is that state politics does not tap the political energies of rural communities. Instead the state insulates itself from the mobilizing issues of rural change in order to protect the interests of the dominant group. This isolation deprives the large political process of energy, enthusiasm and mobilization needed for the changes which broadened welfare and enhanced productivity require. In their different ways, both of these views point to the existence of stress between local communities and the state as well as to stress within the national and local levels of politics. One aim of the later chapters is to sort out the different patterns which political stress can take in Africa and to discuss some of the implications of those patterns. They will address the central question: can the political relationship between state and peasant farmers be placed on a more productive and progressive footing?

There is, however, an important preliminary issue to examine. Our understanding of what is happening in Africa is strongly shaped by the images through which the media filter the information we rely on. Chapter 2 studies the most influential images of the crisis in rural Africa and puts forward a realistic method for avoiding the biases so prevalent in the way news is presented.

∮ 2 ∮

BEYOND THE IMAGES OF
CRISIS

The news media have been quick to project images of crisis in Africa. Whatever our other knowledge of the African reality, media images become implicit reference points for the way all of us, including many Africans, think about Africa's hard times. The images oversimplify and distort reality. By promoting misleading presuppositions they obstruct accurate perception and clear thinking. Discussing them can clarify the assumptions each of us brings to the subject. Examining the images can also help to bring into focus three important dimensions of agricultural communities in Africa: cultural processes, ecological imperatives, and political–economic forces. The three dimensions are important aspects of the broad political economy perspective, discussed later on in this chapter, which guides the analysis in this volume.

MEDIA IMAGES OF AFRICAN CRISES

Written and visual news reports on rural Africa repeatedly return to three images: *tribalism*, often pictured as primitive, atavistic, and violently aggressive; *eco-disaster*, in which hostile natural forces reduce technologically backward people to helpless starvation or (in the case of AIDS) fatal and disheartening illness; *mismanagement* of the economy by governments or social classes depicted as incompetent and exploitative self-servers, who victimize and impoverish rural producers who are striving for a better living.

Tribalism

The television image is one of black people, often of distinctive stature, dress, and language. The Masai warriors in the game park films or the !Kung (Bushmen) in the film *The gods must be crazy* convey the underlying image of rural tribal communities. In the image, authority and leadership, as well as custom, culture, and physiology, unite the group and set it apart from outsiders, who are usually regarded with suspicion and incomprehension. News commentary in print and on the air evokes the same kind of perception: in the 1960s the continuing story was Zaire with its secessions, guerrilla wars, and interventions. In the 1970s Uganda's conflicts were used to bolster the tribal interpretation of African politics. Conflicts in Nigeria, Zimbabwe, Angola, and Sudan have in their turn received similar treatment. Most of us know something of the tensions among Igbo, Yoruba, and Hausa; Shona and Matebele; Ovimbundu and the rest; and Arab northerners and black African southerners. When the conflicts of today die away, it is certain that another venue for the eruption of tribal Africa will be discovered.

Readers and viewers come away with a picture of separate tribal communities that are individually integral and mutually incompatible. Open conflict flares up among the groups and infects their relations with the state, which then becomes repressive either on behalf of one ethnic community against others or else in the name of a supra-ethnic national identity.

Perceiving Africa as a continent of tribal communities is not confined to casual observers; it is part of the analysis of intelligence agencies and academics, and even of African politicians (Rothchild and Olorunsola 1983). It also has a long intellectual and administrative history in the annals of colonial rule and official colonial social science (Mafeje 1971).

To expose the errors and misrepresentations in the whole history of the perception of ethnic Africa is beyond the scope of this book. However, we do need to recognize the importance of cultural variety in Africa and the possibility in most rural communities of several different cultural definitions of political issues and groups. Most local communities are culturally diverse; they cope with that diversity as part of everyday social and political life. Ethnic diversity is often a creative factor in peasant farming communities, reflecting a complex and changing division of labour and the interaction through generations of people over a wide geographic area.

The cultural dimension of community is a process of forming and mediating cultural identities. Ethnic, religious, regional, clan, caste, age, and gender identities may all enter into the formation of partial or encompassing community cultures. They may be the basis on which existing or aspiring leaders make their political claims. They may also form some of the connecting sinews which tie communities together within rural areas and across the rural–urban divide. But it is a grave distortion either to take ethnic identity alone as a sovereign and ineluctable definer of community boundaries and loyalties or to see it as a purely negative, disruptive, and conflictive force. It is useful, however, to ask about the conditions under which cultural identity gains great political salience for rural communities and what the consequences of ethnic politics are for rural communities and state–community relations.

With respect to peasant-farming communities, ethnic loyalties can only be one colour on a multi-colour map.

Gender, age, class, religion, political group, and institutional affiliation also create groups and define lines of conflict.

Eco-disaster

Another telling television image of rural Africa is that of a region devastated by drought whose communities are put to flight in search of a way to survive. Wandering individuals, families, and communities rendered helpless by the forces of nature seek succor from international aid. Disaster creates a new community of suffering to which dedicated donors attempt to minister. The image of eco-disaster takes the concrete form of a refugee camp. The proximate cause of the disaster, in this image, is either dangerously capricious environmental conditions or an imbalance between an agricultural economy and its environment. The climate is changing for the worse or the land is over-farmed and overgrazed because of a combination of population growth and inappropriate techniques of farming. The impression left is one of peasant farming communities whose customs and knowledge are no longer effectual and whose capacity for adaptive change has been exhausted. The implication is that drastic change imposed from outside is the only alternative to death.

Africa's agricultural communities do adapt to their environments; many economic and social features which define rural communities can be traced to such adaptation. However, in their simplified depiction of a tragedy of the moment these images obscure the largely successful adaptation of technique to environment which was achieved in pre-colonial African agriculture. They also discount the life histories of real, active communities trying over years of worsening conditions to maintain a productive base. And they ignore the efforts of communities away from the immediate overwhelming crises of drought and flood to reconstruct their social and economic practice in response to changing ecological realities.

It is now widely acknowledged that the great Sahel famine of 1974–76 resulted from deficient rainfall in a system of production which had been fundamentally altered by the adoption of peanuts and cotton as major cash crops (Franke and Chasin 1980). Trade in food grains also had made it common for families to diminish, sometimes to zero, the amount of basic food grain they would keep in store in case of emergency. More intensive land use and the cultivation of increased marginal land made much of the cultivated land more vulnerable to drought than had previously been the case. Rural communities that lost their control over nature either disintegrated into their constituent families and individuals, each making its own form of retreat, or traded their dependence upon nature for a dependence on government or international donors for food and other aid.

Unexplored by the images of devastation are ecological changes short of disaster which can have deep effects on rural communities. Women go further and further for wood for cooking. Fringe land is brought under cultivation. Cattle are kept further away. All these changes may bring community members into conflict with other communities nearby. In addition, it may be necessary to buy fertilizer to make the land yield, to dig wells in order to have a minimum of water, and to learn the use of new crops and tools. Some members of the community may have to emigrate to find work and if possible to gain income to send back to the community.

A newer image of disaster and helplessness is beginning to take shape: that of a continent afflicted with AIDS and suffering the loss of up to fifty per cent of the population in some areas, while governments lacking funds and personnel are unable to take effective counter-measures. As the

AIDS crisis evolves around the globe, it may become more difficult for non-Africans to see its African component as something distant and alien, but present indications are that the disease will attain disaster-proportions in parts of Africa before it does in other parts of the world. In early 1988 the true dimensions of the problem were still unclear, but African governments were beginning to take measures to slow the spread of the disease (Mann 1987).

Mismanagement and exploitation

A third misleading image of Africa is found on the business pages of newspapers and magazines of the western world. It shows bloated and corrupt or ideologically misguided governments killing the initiatives of farmers and private business by taxing, regulating, and controlling. It highlights the corruption of government officials and the failures of public enterprises. Governments are represented as too undisciplined to halt corruption or limit their own spending on unproductive services and subsidies for urban voters. Worse still, the ideologically misguided try to apply inappropriate forms of socialism and Marxism with particularly devastating effects on rural production. Peasants in this image are naturally suspicious and individualistic. Any effort to socialize them results in sullen impoverishment. And governments are incapable of managing complex and centralized planning and administrative systems.

The only hope for more rational government behaviour, according to the business pages, is the bracing constraint of an IMF or World Bank structural adjustment package, complete with stringent inspections and controls to monitor performance. The governments themselves are hopeless, although the peasant farmers are seen to have the virtue of responding to price incentives. Politically, however, rural people are consistently seen as helpless before the unscrupulous power of the urban classes who find ways to manipulate prices, monopolize access to goods, enforce taxes, and suppress or deflect resistance and opposition.

The image directs attention to the way in which higher political, economic, and military powers define or attempt to define the conditions of existence of rural communities. Systems of taxation, administration, crop pricing, and patronage do shape the structures and boundaries of rural communities. But communities are not defenceless against such impositions, and the impositions themselves must conform to the cultural and ecological dimensions of the community in question. Here is another image which derives its persuasiveness from a partial insight which, on its own, marks a serious distortion.

Errors in the images

The common images of crisis in rural Africa are all one-sided and profoundly misleading. The images of rampant tribal conflict, of complete ecological breakdown, and of massive managerial incompetence and exploitation err in conveying a sense of inert helplessness on the part of rural Africans. The images become dangerous because of the action they imply. Picturing a violent and primordial tribal morass leads to a policy of waiting for a change of generations. The image of an ecological disaster suggests that a whole new system of production and therefore a new social system must be created. The idea of exploitative mismanagement confines the remedy to the bracing purity of market forces and managerial training. It ignores the forms of social and economic power to which governments respond and the less-than-glorious record of business-managed markets in the colonial period.

There is a real struggle going on among influential groups to bolster and to project each of these images. The objective is to instill a certain perspective, a definite bias, in the commonsense ideas which are necessarily the starting point of debate in the mass media and of discussion in more restricted and more influential circles of policy makers. It does make a difference whether or not the World Bank succeeds in pinning the label of inept and self-serving economic managers of their rural economies on Africa's governments or if public opinion in Africa begins to see peasant farmers as an exploited class.

The images are durable partly because they feed the interests and predilections of powerful groups, and partly because they each contain important elements of reality. The perspective of political economy attempts to ground analysis in a realistic appraisal of all the important forces and circumstances shaping peasant farming in Africa. The perspective recognizes cultural difference, ecological processes, and the possibility of exploitation, but does not fall into the trap of reducing analysis to the adoption of a single misleading and oversimplified image.

A BROAD POLITICAL ECONOMY

The mass media's images of crisis in Africa – rampant tribalism, relentless eco-disaster, debilitating mismanagement, and rapacious exploitation – may all be crude distortions and hopelessly misleading as guides for designing policy; but they are durable. That they all can claim some correspondence to the reality of at least some regions helps to explain their persistence. They are also strengthened in each case by more detailed and professional versions. The kind of political economy which guides the presentation in this book can help get beyond the impasse of simplified images. It stresses organization of production, the pattern of community, the process of accumulation, and the structures of power. Its focus is interplay among production, politics, ideas of value and meaning, and the environment.

Politics in this book is taken to mean discussion, conflict, and decision about matters of common concern in a group or community. State politics gathers together important issues and powerful means of action and enforcement backed by concentrated police powers and administrative organization. However, in its own more confined sphere there can be a meaningful politics of family production units, of villages, and of other kinds of coɪ ᷣunities (Leftwich 1983).

A great deal of politics has to do with the repair and adjustment of social and economic relations, usually in such a way as to conserve the economic and political power of the already dominant group under changing circumstances. Rural communities under economic and cultural stress are fertile ground for political tension and conflict. Challenges to existing authority, questioning of old patterns by younger people, and tensions about how to cope with such issues as the absorption of new immigrants, growing population pressure on available land, or how to fight for government spending can erupt into local political fights and crises.

The perspective of this book, then, is one which stresses the active efforts toward political construction under conditions which are often very difficult. The political builders are found in governments and throughout the state apparatus, of course, but they are also found in villages and local communities based on region, culture or interest. They are even found in families trying to arrange their economic and political relations so as to survive and prosper. Transnational agencies – from the World Bank and the IMF, to the development assistance branches of European and North American governments, to transnational corporations, and to agencies of political and economic manipulation and sabotage – also have their agendas of political construction and destruction. The aim of the book is to give some understanding of how this variety of often conflicting activities and efforts gains expression in peasant farming communities and in their relationship with government.

The relevant history for understanding peasant farming communities in Africa is a long one, encompassing periods of state formation and of installation of forms of social, cultural and economic dominance which long pre-date colonialism. Therefore, this book will sometimes invoke past events and the historical depth of current processes, but it makes no claim to being a historical study.

Despite the broad and diverse nature of the forces of rural change in Africa, the relationship between state and peasant farming communities is a strategic focal point. Many of the forces of change flow through this relationship. The government collects taxes, sets official crop prices, undertakes local administration, and implements development policies and projects. All these activities impinge upon individual lives, group patterns, and class relationships structured in communities of different kinds. Rural individuals, groups, classes, and communities in their turn act upon the central government and its local arms and agencies. Rural people may also try to evade the government's regulations and to thwart its intentions. State–community relations are therefore crucial for the ways in which both states and communities serve the needs and interests of their populations.

PEASANT FARMING AS A KIND OF PRODUCTION

To understand the dynamics in question, refined definitions and precise concepts are in order. Not every kind of agriculture counts as peasant farming. Self-provisioning is a part of the production system of peasant farmers, but in its pure form it is quite distinct. Pure self-provisioning (production by a kinship group for its own use and for local barter) was a historic reality in many parts of Africa, and there still exist a few regions remote from or abandoned by markets and a few marginalized farms where agriculture proceeds with little reference to markets. Such regions are very rare; even where cultivators produce crops without purchased inputs for their own use and not for sale, they usually also send part of the available farm labour away for wage employment in mines, plantations, or construction. They are producing and selling labour as their cash crop equivalent. The off-farm labour market is another dimension of integration in the wider system of production similar in many ways to peasant farming.

Pastoralism (raising and herding cattle, sheep, and goats) is not the same as peasant farming, although where milk and meat are sold pastoralists have much in common with peasant farmers. Yet, their mobility, their special relationship to the land, and their intricate social forms of ownership of cattle give specialized cattle herders a distinctiveness which requires analysis in its own terms. There is evidence that pastoralists in West Africa are cultivating more subsistence crops on permanent homesteads; they are becoming semi-pastoralists or peasant farmers with a strong interest in livestock. Of course a large number of peasant farmers also keep cattle, often as an activity quite separate from farming (Eicher and Baker 1982, 164).

Nor are hunting and gathering or collecting and capturing food from the wild the same as peasant farming. As a mode of production, hunting and gathering supports communities which are typically much smaller, more mobile, and more egalitarian than peasant farming communities. In Africa today there are no more than a few thousand members of hunting and gathering communities. However, peasant farmers do harvest wild foods; in times of crop failure or economic hardship especially, collecting and hunting may become a vital and indispensable source of nourishment.

Also distinct from peasant farming is plantation agriculture, in which centrally-managed large-scale units of agricultural production hire labour to carry out work on crops like sugar cane, pineapple, rubber, and tea (Beckford 1972). Of course the plantation workers may be peasant farmers away from their farms on contract. In some cases a plantation or a processing and marketing company will contract with peasant farmers to grow and harvest a crop under considerable supervision. Such examples of contract farming are useful in raising the issue of the kind of control over production itself which can be exercised by the agencies which supply inputs to the farm and which purchase its crop. Where does peasant farming become a form of wage labour?

Peasant farming defined

Peasant farming is taken in this book to mean farming with hoes and animal-drawn ploughs or other simple equipment, using mainly family labour, producing a significant proportion of the basic consumption needs of the local community; while purchasing some consumption goods and some agricultural inputs, and selling some local products, outside the community. The text avoids using the terms 'peasant' and 'peasantry' without the qualifier 'farming' or 'farmer'. The mention of farming offsets the pejorative resonance which 'peasant' holds for many people and serves as a reminder that participation in commercial markets is an important part of the work of almost all agricultural producers in rural Africa.

	Small-scale commodity producers use family labour to produce crops for sale, not to meet their own needs directly.	
Pure self-provisioners sell no crop and achieve self-sufficiency through very local exchange.	Peasant farmers farm the land, mainly with family labour, using simple equipment, providing directly for many of their needs, and selling some of their production.	Capitalist farmers sell almost all their crop and hire most of their labour.
	Wage workers sell their labour as their main source of income and engage in agriculture only as a minor sideline	

Figure 1 Peasant-farming and related economic units

As farmers, peasant farmers are strongly influenced by markets. They pay attention to the price they must pay for essential inputs, for transporting their crop to the point of sale, and for seasonal labour. They relate such costs to the price they receive for the crop. Often, they know how far the price they receive departs from the official national price, and they may have a rough idea of how it compares to the world price. How price changes influence their farming and political activity is a much-debated question. In cases where alternative sources of cash income are weak or absent, falling prices for their products may not induce peasant farmers to grow less. Part of the analysis of this book will consider the way peasant farmers are linked to markets.

In a conceptually pure typology of productive units, peasant farming fits only awkwardly (Friedmann 1980). It has boundaries with four other types (Figure 1). On one side peasant farming shades into pure self-provisioning, where nothing is produced for sale. On a second side it shades into small-scale market production or petty commodity production as more and more of the product is produced for sale rather than for direct use. On a third side peasant farming shades into capitalist farming, as family labour and animal power give way to machine power and hired workers. On a fourth side peasant farming shades into labour supply or proletarianization, as members of the unit spend more and more of their time working for wages in nearby or distant labour markets. Real peasant farming units straddle and combine these alternatives in various and changing combinations. The adaptability of their integration with wider productive systems is an important aspect of the resilience of peasant farming in Africa. Some observers think it is also a reason for their failure to make rapid increases in productivity.

Peasant farming communities

The rural communities of greatest interest for this book share a basic and vital economic dependence on peasant farming as the main source of income for most of their inhabitants. It should be remembered, however, that many other occupations are present: communities can include farm workers, cattle herders, merchants, money-lenders, government extension agents, administrators, carpenters, masons, beauticians, smiths, leather workers, weavers, potters, equipment repairers, police, tailors, and many others. These occupations may be combined with farming, and they often are. Farmers, of course, may be larger or smaller operators and some may hire labour. Usually many of the other occupations are services to the farming population.

Peasant farming can be combined with a large variety of occupations within the rural community or, in the case of seasonal employment, at quite long distances. The peasant farmer who moves by choice or constraint into farm labour or carpentry for more than half of the family income, and begins to think of himself or herself as a worker or carpenter, remains a part-time peasant farmer. The fact that the category shades at the edges into self-provisioning, commercial farming, wage labour, and skilled trades means that the cultural importance of peasant farming for the community may be even greater than its real economic weight suggests, and that the group that identifies itself with the values of peasant farming is larger than the group of peasant farmers proper.

Peasant farmers are also strongly related to their local society. They are linked by marriage and kinship to surrounding families. Through community ties they may recruit help with farming operations, find social and economic obligations imposed upon them, get food in time of need, or combine to raise investment capital. The economic and political activity of peasant farmers is better understood if it is related to the relevant community context.

Depending on the questions being asked, the type and size of the community chosen for discussion can vary (Esman and Uphoff 1984). For this book the most important kind of rural community is geo-political; it has a territorial location and a political structure, and over a typical year it encompasses most of the living time of most of its members. The smallest kind of rural community is the village of several or a few dozen farming units and a population of fifty to two hundred. In a few places the primary villages may be considerably larger, with populations of several hundred. Whatever its size, the village community has a recognized boundary and a corporate organization, and often an obvious geographic unity.

The most inclusive rural community would be a district or other organized and recognized ecological and social region uniting a population of up to several thousand people in a common social economy. The unity of the larger community may be one of a shared social pattern or of a more dynamic integration based on division of labour as well as shared administration and territory. It usually includes recognition or self-identification of the community by most of its members. The smaller definition of community helps to reveal the densest forms of collective life in which peasant farmers engage and which play an important role in the viability of rural economies. The larger definition brings into the picture the presence of government offices and officials, the working machinery of government policy, and the efforts of rural people to influence government. It is also sometimes useful to single out other specialized communities not based on locality but defined by a cultural, religious, or linguistic identity. In this book such cultural communities are always identified by their particular defining feature.

Africa's peasant farming communities differ in important ways, as will be shown in later chapters; for example, in the density of population, the availability of uncultivated arable land, and settlement in scattered homesteads or in concentrated villages or towns. Yet there are important common features of rural African society: low material standards of living, high proportion of income in kind from local sources, emphasis on kinship in the patterning of social relationships, reliance on human energy for transport and production, reliance on strong local skills for a wide range of essential economic and cultural activities (construction, agriculture, stock-rearing, moral and social education, ceremonial activity), and rapid social change. It is the character of the complex of social changes that makes the current period especially crucial for rural Africa.

At the centre of many important changes are the peasant farmers themselves. It will be useful to have a clearer picture of peasant farms and the way they work.

§ 3 §

CHANGING PEASANT FARMS

There is no such thing as a typical peasant farm: the social relations among members of the unit are often complex and the very boundaries of the unit itself are far from clear-cut. The form of integration into wider markets for land, crops, labour, and consumption goods also varies. Diversity and flexibility help to explain the remarkable tenacity of peasant farming under a variety of ecological and political-economic conditions – from semi-arid savannas to equatorial forests, and from socialist institutions to laissez-faire regimes. Variability and complexity contribute to the durability of peasant farming, but they make the tasks of description and analysis more difficult. They even lie at the root of some of the theoretical and policy debates about 'the African peasantry'; writers with differing perspectives sometimes refer to markedly dissimilar peasant farming communities. Clear analysis, therefore, requires a firm conceptual starting point. A benchmark model of a peasant farming unit will help to establish the language for discussing variation. The model is consistent with the definition offered in the last chapter, but it is not itself a definition.

In the simplest case a core group united by family ties shares a living space, farms a set of fields with simple tools, and uses the product of the farm for consumption and for earning cash income. Still in its simplest form, the family lives in a homestead where the tools are kept and which is located in the midst of the fields it farms or in a nearby small village. It is this densely interrelated and compact social unit which is usually assumed to be typical of peasant farming. However, this assumption is mistaken in the case of Africa. Instead the compact peasant family model should be taken as an aid to defining the terms of variation in real peasant-farming units.

The room for variation is apparent when the model is broken down into its constituent elements and key relationships. The elements include a group of people, a living space, a set of tools, and some plots of land. The key relationships are ties uniting the group, property rights giving access to land and tools, a work regime which organizes the group's labour on the land and using the tools, and a method for allocating the product of the work. In addition there is a set of more or less intensive exchanges with external markets and ties of control and participation with external powers.

One set of variations concerns the land. The dwelling land and the farming land may be at some distance from each other, and the farming land may be divided in non-contiguous fields. The dwellings of a single village may be gathered in compact settlements in the midst of the village lands, or they may be scattered in neighbourhood clusters or individual farmsteads. The land farmed by one peasant farming unit may be an assemblage of plots with different kinds of claims on them, some owned, some borrowed, some rented, and some share-cropped. Moreover, the group that shares land rights, the group that lives together, the group that shares ownership of tools, and the group that farms together may not coincide. Their memberships may differ slightly or decidedly. The degree to which people in the peasant-farming unit actually operate as a unit also varies: they may constitute a centrally managed team deploying land, labour, and tools under common control or they may be a loose collection of individuals or subgroups, each one working quite separately. The ways in which the product or income of the members of the unit are divided can also differ in method of sharing and in the resulting pattern of distribution. In other words, the values and rules in terms of which the production unit manages itself can vary. The relationships of exchange and influence with outside powers also differ enormously. Their changes are major forces in the shaping of Africa's rural political economy.

All of these variations can distinguish different peasant-farming regions, different units within one region, or the same unit at different times.

In later chapters, variations and changes of several kinds will be discussed. In this chapter, two examples of production units, one from Tanzania and one from Senegal, are discussed.

TWO PEASANT-FARMING FAMILIES

Described below are two peasant-farming units from two very different regions. The coffee and maize farming family in the highland area in southwestern Tanzania is described as it was in 1972. The account is taken from a research report on his own family written by a student at the University of Dar es Salaam, as part of a larger research project on prospects for the formation of communal villages in the area. The report was written about a year before the government compelled most rural people to live in planned villages. The description of the millet and groundnut (or peanut) farm in Senegal comes from the work of technicians who work for the Société de Développement et de Vulgarisation Agricole (SODEVA), a government extension and research organization in Senegal. The case noted here was one recorded in 1983 in the region of Kaolack, a part of the groundnut zone which had not been disastrously affected by drought. The data recorded reflect the agroeconomic interests of SODEVA in ways of improving the productive efficiency of individual farms. The examples show how wide the differences among farming units can be; they also reveal how 'objective' description reflects the orientation of the case authors.

A coffee and maize farmer in Tanzania

The household has 17 members. The father and head of the household has three wives, all of them mothers with children. None of the children is married. The head of the household is 45 years old and the wives are 38, 30, and 25 years old respectively. There are four sons aged 22, 15, 7, and 3; and nine daughters aged 12, 11, 11, 9, 6, 3, 2, 2, and 2 weeks.

Only the four parents are engaged in farming throughout the year. Six children are in school: the eldest son at university, the next son in secondary school, and four daughters in primary school.

Only in the coffee fields does the household work on commonly owned holdings. Usually the head of the household divides the coffee fields equally among his three wives. Hence each mother will have contributed equally by the time she has finished her portion of the coffee fields. The head of the household collects the money from coffee sales and pays out equal portions to the mothers. There is no fixed wage since income from sales depends upon the quantity produced and the prices fetched on the market. In 1970 the family received about Shs. (shillings) 3000 and each mother got about 50. The rest was managed by the head of the household. He used it for paying off loans to the cooperative society for fertilizer, insecticide, and other farm inputs; for the children's school fees and school uniforms; and for his own expenses.

The father of the family organizes work in the coffee holdings, making it the first priority among farming tasks. He checks the quality of weeding in the holdings; if any wife shows some slacking, he urges her to work harder.

Although the food crops are the concern of the individual wives, in some years the head of the household organizes cultivation of his own food garden for emergencies such as food shortages. His wives take his food garden as their second priority after coffee and work it in cooperative groups. Some of the crop is used in preparing a feast for collective work groups. Surplus food crops harvested in the head's fields may be sold for money.

No one in the household works for wages outside the household, although some do participate in the exchange of collective work. The household receives labour from outside in three ways: seasonal wage employment, *ujima*, and the *kibarua* system (Mushi 1971). Of the three methods the *ujima* form of cooperation is the most effective. One of the mothers prepares beer and in collaboration with the head of the household asks relatives and friends to help. Usually these people are non-Christians, for no one in the family believes in Christianity. Christians in earlier days shunned the preparation and drinking of beer and therefore would not participate. *Ujima* is used when large-scale or heavier and urgent tasks need to be done in the shortest time possible, such as clearing millet fields by felling the large trees of the *miomba* woodlands on steep mountain slopes. This is considered to be men's work. Other types of work in which *ujima* is used include weeding, spraying, and picking coffee; these are jobs done by both sexes. On food crop fields, especially for weeding and harvesting of millet, *ujima* work is usually done by women only. Women sometimes use food as payment for *ujima* work. The work is arranged so that invitations to the same cooperating group do not clash, and so that some days are left for members to work on their own fields.

Employing workers for two to three months during the cultivation period for coffee used to be common. The labourers came in from a neighbouring area where they had no cash crops or were drawn from recent settlers in the area who had yet to establish their own cash crops. They were paid about Shs. 45 for the season, an amount which also happened to be the annual personal tax levied on adults at the end of the colonial period. Construction work in the area on the pipeline, the road, and the railway employed workers at a higher wage, making it hard to find seasonal workers.

Kibarua refers to day labour or piece work paid either in cash or in such goods as sugar or salt. For weeding a worker is paid in goods, for example a litre of salt for weeding five coffee trees. Coffee picking is paid in cash, from Shs. 0.5 to Shs. 1 for a 5 gallon tin of coffee, depending on the pressure to get the berries picked and on the competition for labour from other farms, especially the few European-owned farms left in the area.

The land owned by the family was acquired simply by claiming a piece of empty land. In those days people were far apart and one had only to approach the chief for permission to farm empty land. Now the family also plants some millet fields on the common land on the mountain slope. No terms or payments are imposed and the different families reach agreements about the location of boundaries. After harvest these fields revert to common ownership. Some are far away, as shifting cultivation is still practised on the common fields. Recently the family bought a coffee farm of some two acres, about two miles distant from the homestead in a place where the rainfall is more reliable than it is on the household lands.

Coffee is the only cash crop. Food crops when in surplus may be sold, but this happens rarely. The main food crops are millet, maize, cassava, and beans, although there are many others. The coffee fields total about twelve acres. Production varies from 500 to 800 kilograms and fetches Shs. 2000 to Shs. 3000 (in the period 1968 to 1972). Fertilizer for the coffee costs about Shs. 450; copper sulphate (a fungicide) costs about Shs. 688. The family buys both on credit at the cooperative where the coffee is later marketed. Food crop fields total about 18 acres; they are widely scattered plots and no effort is made to intensify production. Most years the stored food runs out before the new crops are ready to harvest and some food staples have to be purchased. The family annually produces about 10 bags of millet, 4 bags of cassava, and 3 bags of maize, plus much additional maize eaten green from the field.

In her own food crop production each wife cultivates fields which she owns, working with considerable autonomy. Yet the head of the household may advise his wives about what to grow in their food plots, and he sees to it that they grow enough food.

The family's three bulls were sent away to be kept by a relative, because the boys of herding-age are in school.

A peanut and millet farmer in Senegal

The household is a small one with only four members. The head of the household came to the Birkelane area from Guinea (Conakry) a number of years ago as a *surga*, or a dependant attached to a household who works for the head of the household in return for the use of some land on his own account. Recently he married a woman from Guinea and began a part-time business as a small trader. They have an infant child. Although he still lives in the concession with his former *nyatigué*, or master, he is now regarded as a head of household with a separate production unit.

During the farming season he works in his fields in the morning and the afternoon, but at midday he sells rice, matches, salt, paraffin, tea, tinned milk, and other small items of current consumption from his house. He gets his supplies from nearby market towns. His wife works in the fields, and now he has as his own *surga* the young son of a prominent man in the village.

The head of the household still gets much help from his former *nyatigué* and in return still does some work in the latter's fields. They work more or less as partners.

The family farms about five hectares, half of it in groundnuts. The agricultural income of the production unit, almost entirely from groundnut sales, came in 1981–82 to about 180,000 CFA francs (the currency of the Communauté Financière Africaine which is pegged to the French franc – 1 franc CFA = .02 French francs). Personal taxes and farming expenses at the cooperative came to about 30,000 CFA francs. Millet production was about 1,860 kilograms. Of this 10 per cent was given in *assaka*, or tithes, to a Muslim organization. According to government norms, 140 kilograms of cereal per person is an adequate dietary staple. By that standard this family has a substantial surplus of millet. They also had a carryover stock of about 500 kilograms from previous years. Valuing the grain at 50 francs per kilogram, the total farming income of the unit is about 240,000 CFA francs or 60,000 CFA francs per person. At official exchange rates that is between $200 and $300. SODEVA figures indicate that there was additional groundnut production that was not marketed through official channels, and there is no account in the case study of earnings from small retail trade.

FOCUS ON THE FARMING UNITS

Peasant farming is not a simple activity. Even when rather simple tools like hoes, knives, and axes are the mechanical instruments of production and when human energy is the main power source, peasant farmers employ great skill in choosing cultivars, arranging fields, scheduling work activities, and applying specific rules of planting and tending crops. A single farm may combine scattered fields in several different farming zones, pull labour from a wide network of community and kin relations, spread risks through mutual support relations, and invest for security and prestige in cattle and in wider social commitments. Only recently have researchers fully appreciated the detailed skill in ecological adaptation and the intensive ability in the management of social relations which peasant farming demands. It is no wonder that agricultural economists adduce a mysterious management or skill factor to account for a large part of the variation in the productivity of farmers operating under similar conditions. Especially under conditions of change in markets, social relations, and agricultural practices, management in the broad micro-political sense is predictably important for economic performance.

Yet much more than managerial sophistication is involved in the complexity of peasant farming. In peasant farming there is a large overlap in three distinct functions: production, consumption, and reproduction. As *producers*, peasant farmers mix labour and other inputs with land to create goods for home consumption (use values) and for sale (exchange values). As *consumers*, peasant farmers make use of the food, housing, clothing, and other goods they themselves produce, and they purchase goods in local and long distance trade. As *reproducers*, peasant farming units, particularly their women members, create and rear children to take their place in the production system and in the society. They also often seek to maintain conditions for their own continued existence, trying in times of change to keep making a living in the way that is familiar to them, sometimes explicitly defending a culture or way of life, and sometimes simply trying to survive. The impressive resilience of export crop regions is evidence for purposeful persistence of peasant-farming communities. (Of course individuals and farming families do abandon farming when it is impossible to continue or when the balance of opportunity clearly favours change. Whole regional communities always seem to seek compromises which allow them to continue, except under the most extreme duress.)

Economic science usually divides these functions. Reflecting the specialization that is common in industrial societies, it analyses production as if it were the exclusive activity of a specialized social unit, as it tends to be for factories and shops. It takes consumption as the main economic activity of households and it leaves reproduction, also a household function, to the demographers and educationists. Such a division violates the real integration of activities in peasant farming communities. Instead we need to consider production, consumption, and reproduction together, recognizing the fact that they are the joint occupation of peasant farmers. One of the advantages of political economy and economic anthropology (particularly in their Marxist versions) on which the analysis that follows draws, is the explicit combination of these functions in a single sweep of analysis.

From this combined standpoint the key elements in the peasant-farming unit are land, inputs, people-as-labour (labour power), people-as-reproducers (child-bearing women), products for consumption, products for sale, money, and people-as-consumers (consumption needs).

For a peasant-farming community to survive, these elements must be combined in such a way that production takes place, needs are met, children are born and shaped to fill the places left open by illness and death, wanted goods are produced or purchased, and enough products or labour are sold to pay for purchases. To get all these variables to fit together in a manner that satisfies basic social values, reflects individual drives and differences, and allows for cultural expression is a major social task requiring much intricate social labour and much political work.

As peasant farming units simultaneously face the three tasks of production, consumption, and reproduction they generate a lively internal politics and, like other workplaces, establish their own small political regime. The micro-politics of peasant farming becomes part of the analysis of rural change in Africa. The exercise of power, the forms of conflict, and the terms of political discussion in peasant-farming units and communities fit together with economic relations, but they are not reducible to them. There is need for an explicit micro-political analysis.

Production

The factors of peasant farming production are land, labour, and other inputs (tools, seed, fertilizer, and chemicals). All of them have been profoundly affected by the market system, yet land and labour, by far more important than other inputs, have rarely become full commodities to be exchanged purely on the basis of supply and demand.

Land. Although there is a market for land in many parts of rural Africa, rural communities seem to resist full market relations in land. In precolonial Africa the residual rights in land were vested in the community (defined as village, ethnic group, chiefdom, kin-group or territorial group). The right to use land for construction of a house or for cultivation was usually allocated by a community authority; often a chief, a village council of elders, or a special land chief. The right of usage was usually inheritable and was passed from father to son (or to sister's son in matrilineal descent). In most areas cultivable land was not in short supply and the pressures on the allocation institutions were not enormous. Often the receiver of the right to use land made a symbolic gift to the chief who was guardian of communal rights. In any given year families might lend and borrow the use of fields; in this way the use of land was distributed roughly according to the ability to use it. In many African societies there were categories of people whose rights to land were weaker, indirect, or nonexistent. Slaves, for example, usually had to seek land from their masters, and strangers from outside the community needed special permission from the chief or council empowered to allocate land.

With cash payment playing a part in more and more transactions, it is not surprising that the right to use land has become a partial commodity to be rented or even sold. Symbolic tribute paid to a chief comes to resemble the payment of rent to a landlord, and also to reflect market forces. Although custom and law may disapprove, rights to use land may in fact be bought and sold, sometimes clandestinely. Such sales are sometimes justified as sales of improvements on the land, not sale of the land itself, but the effect is to make land a commodity.

A few governments, notably that of Kenya, have tried to encourage the treatment of land as private property subject to markets. Kenya legislated full freehold tenure for agricultural land with registered titles, and full rights to sell. Other governments have abolished private ownership of agricultural land, making it national or state property, and created local committees to oversee the allocation of rights to use land. The working of such committees may in fact allow and even encourage market transactions in land, perhaps with certain controls. However, even where free-hold tenure is the legal framework for allocation of land and even where *de facto* markets in land are well established, the influence of kinship obligations on the allocation of land can still be strong. In Kenya's settlement schemes,it was observed in the 1970s that poor farmers on small plots accepted landless kin on to their land, while richer farmers on large plots often purchased land for their less fortunate relatives (Leo 1984, 165). Within their rights of ownership, freeholders loan the use of land to relatives more or less as custom dictates.

In the early 1970s sale prices of land in Tanzania's Ismani District, where maize was grown for the domestic market, were equivalent to about two years' rent, because such transfers were not secure and contravened customary law (Awiti 1975, 68–69). In a number of places chiefs or land chiefs have succeeded in turning rights to allocate land or to hold it for the community into full rights of personal ownership. And some farm land which has been developed commercially is treated by business-oriented owners and the law as an extension of urban land, which is a matter for capitalist investment and management.

In some localities there is a lack of consistency and clarity in the rules about access to land. Customary rights with some recognition given to supply-and-demand forces is a frequent pattern. What it often means in practice is a degree of ambiguity about land rights and the possibility of appeal to conflicting rules. Verbal adherence to customary rules which guarantee access to land to every member of the community may mask the taking over of much land by the rich and the powerful. In the case of large government-sponsored agricultural schemes, pre-existing rights and rules may be set aside completely as new government-created rules are enforced. In any particular case, local inquiry must be made to find out the current state of the contention among customary claims, market force, and government regulations.

Labour. The second critical factor of peasant-farming production is labour. Most of it usually comes from the members of the household and from exchanges household members make with other kin or members of the local community. As with land, however, the market has affected the recruitment of labour, sometimes very profoundly. The most widespread influence is the replacement of labour exchange with wage labour.

In most peasant-farming systems there are seasons of high labour demand, usually planting (when it is imperative to get seeds in the ground following the onset of the rains, in order to get full advantage of a limited growing season) and harvest (when delay may lead to substantial loss of crop due to shattering, bird damage, or decay). Before markets were very important, many societies had institutions of labour exchange in which teams of kin or friends, or age-mates helped one another, sometimes in return for a beer party or a feast. The exchange of labour often favoured the big farmers who could afford more feasts and who needed more labour, but the flow did not follow market forces or principles. Once the need and opportunity for earning a wage were present, the work parties tended to decrease in frequency. Farmers had to find other ways of recruiting labour. Wage labour, work in return for a share of the crop (sharecropping), or work in return for the right to use some land (labour rental) were all instituted in different places and in different combinations. In a few places the penetration of the market principle has been so profound as to control the recruitment of labour from within the household. Heads of families in some parts of Sudan pay their wives and children a wage for work done on the home farm in order to compete with the earning opportunities on nearby cotton schemes (Ali and O'Brien 1984, 231).

Control of labour has changed in another way as well. The chance to gain disposable income from farming induces young people to set up their own separate farming units earlier than they otherwise would have done. Where elders have been able to retain their control and resist the fragmentation of the farming unit, the internal pressures within the household are made more intense. In Northern Nigeria, where production is still organized in large extended family units or big houses, it is common for young men of the house to simply disappear, usually during the night (Hill 1972, 1977). They depart to seek their fortune elsewhere, without taking leave or asking permission. They lose both the oppression and the secure identity of family membership in return for the freedom to seek employment in the urban labour market.

Other inputs.   Most writing on Africa's rural economy does not regard other inputs as important variable factors in peasant-farming production. It is assumed that most farmers can make or buy the basic tools of hoe and machete and that they save the seed they need. However, even where new inputs are not used, the old ones can pose a significant barrier to entry into farming, even where land is available. A young family may not have the hoe, the knife, the seed, and the food to live on, needed to clear and plant a farm. And savings or material is needed to build a house. In some regions many families are 'too poor to farm', largely because they cannot afford the other inputs (Hill 1972). Other evidence of the importance of basic tools in peasant farming comes from Mozambique, where a precipitous decline in output from family farms in the mid 1980s is partly attributed to the inadequate supply of the most basic tools: hoes and machetes.

With the change in methods of production, the other inputs take on a much larger role in differentiation among peasant farming units. Some studies have regarded the possession of oxen and ploughs or tractors as the major criteria to distinguish peasants from small farmers and capitalist farmers. One study in Zambia found that the different means of production correlate with the organization and operation of the unit (Momba 1982). Hoe farmers often sell some of their labour to larger farmers, and they also sell a small proportion of their crop. Plough farmers are self-sufficient in labour and they sell more of their crop. The tractor farmers hire labour and produce mainly to sell, trying to expand their operations. As more research and investment goes into agriculture in Africa, the importance of the 'other inputs' will become much more significant.

Purchased inputs already constitute a major lever of control over production in some places. Where farmers do not themselves produce and retain a basic input, their whole operation is vulnerable to the supplier of that input. In many of the cash-crop zones, a pattern of credit has long been established in which peasant farmers must take seed on credit at the beginning of the growing season, only to repay it (along with other debts) at interest during harvest time. A poor crop due to poor distribution of rains, illness in the family, or a plague of birds or grasshoppers can reduce a farming unit to begging. The lender can use the leverage obtained to control the method of production and to extract payments so heavy that they endanger the most basic livelihood of the producers, as has occurred in Sudan's Kordofan province among growers of peanuts and sesame (Elmekki 1985). In some cases agricultural credit and technical assistance agencies have tried to use credit controls as a lever to change farming practices.

More often the controls are used to divert income from farming into the hands of the lenders. As the use of inputs becomes more widespread and critical for production, the vulnerability of farmers to the suppliers of the inputs and of the credit to purchase them will become greater. As will be discussed below, some analysts believe that such outside controls are essential for more productive farming in Africa. Others argue that peasant farmers need more effective countervailing economic and social power.

Changes in the factors of production.   It is frequently observed that the techniques of production in African agriculture have not changed qualitatively since before the colonial era. Peasant farmers still cultivate with hoes on small plots. Although the use of new crops, new varieties of old crops, fertilizer, animal traction, tractors, herbicides, and pesticides is more widespread than many imagine, it remains true that neither the mechanical revolution nor the green revolution has brought widespread qualitative change to Africa's agriculture (Eicher and Baker 1982). Yet economic and social changes in the villages of Africa in the past generation or two have been enormous. The ways in which land, labour, and other factors are brought together have changed enormously throughout Africa's peasant-farming communities. Markets and government loans, roads and railroads, research institutions and agricultural extension agencies have all contributed to the changes on the farms themselves. Not only has production been altered, but the very shape of peasant farms and the form of peasant-farming communities have both been profoundly altered, as consideration of consumption and reproduction begin to show.

Consumption
Self-provisioning, or production for own consumption, is a central part of the definition of peasant production

units. Certainly in Africa most peasant farmers produce a large part of the food they consume, as well as the fuel, housing, and furniture they use. At the same time, crucial items in their consumption basket are usually purchased: cooking oil, salt, soap, lighting fuel, tea, cloth, pots and pans, and sewing needles. In the period before harvest, many peasant-farming families are short of food, having used their stored grains and having spent their meagre cash reserve. They often purchase a basic starchy staple on credit. Sometimes price and import policies make it easier and cheaper to buy imported rice than to buy local millet.

Consumption patterns create links outside the production unit; links of credit and local trade. There are also questions about distribution within the consumption unit. Do men or women control access to the granary? Do men eat first and best while women and children eat what remains? The answers to such questions help explain the way malnutrition is distributed within consumption units under food stress. Case studies show that children and women, who often eat only after the men have finished eating, suffer from malnutrition when men do not. The control and deployment of cash reserves, also often controlled by senior men, shapes opportunities for schooling.

Self-provisioning. The word 'subsistence', when applied to farming, has two distinct meanings: production for own sustenance and making a bare living. Some peasant farmers who provide directly for a large part of their basic needs are not poor in nutrition, clothing, and shelter. And many agriculturalists who rely heavily on market exchange to meet some of their needs are nonetheless barely sustaining themselves. Here the topic fits the first meaning, and to avoid ambiguity the term 'self-provisioning' is used in this book.

One of the critical questions about peasant farmers is their ability to provide for their own basic needs. Some argue that the necessity to engage in cash-crop farming has pushed farmers to neglect production for their own basic needs. In order to grow peanuts or cotton, growers plant less land to millet or maize, spend less time weeding, and reap a smaller food harvest. Although there are examples of such a direct relationship (as when a record cotton harvest coincided with record grain imports in the Sahel in 1983–84), a stronger general argument is made (Timberlake 1985, 73):

Cash crops can combine with population growth to encourage farmers to overcultivate the declining areas reserved for food, or to cultivate them poorly and at the wrong time, or to neglect them. All these factors can result in land degradation – and hunger.

In response, others argue that the roads and fertilizers which encourage cash-crop farming also improve food crop productivity and that farmers only displace food crops with cash crops if the marginal income from the cash crop is greater. By growing more coffee, farmers will increase their cash income sufficiently to be able to buy more maize than they could have grown had they not grown the extra coffee (World Bank 1981, 62–63).

The general point is that the benefits of a changing, dynamic agriculture are not restricted to a single crop or sets of crops. When change accelerates, the productivity of the whole farming system also increases.

This debate is in part a result of attending to data from different kinds of farming areas: the dry-grain farming zones and the wetter tree-crop zones. In the dry zones the cash crops (peanuts, cotton, and sesame) compete quite directly for labour against the food crops (millets, sorghums, and maize), especially in crucial peak periods of planting, weeding, and harvesting. Beyond a certain maximum intensity of labour use, further emphasis on the cash crops will diminish food crop production, and vice versa. In forest tree-crop zone (where coffee, tea, and cocoa are the cash crops; yams and plantains the staple-food crops) the labour peaks are different and there is less direct competition for labour (Tosh 1980).

Purchased necessities. The goods which peasant-farming families purchase are by no means all luxuries. The cash economy is not an overlay upon a self-sufficient, self-provisioning economy. Often basic goods like salt, cooking oil, sugar, tea, pots, cloth, hoes, lighting fuel, and roofing material are purchased. If, for reasons of poverty, a family cannot buy essential food and tools, the whole enterprise of production is threatened. In a number of farming regions seed, especially for cash crops, is purchased each year, often from a government supply agency. Inability to buy seed may interrupt cash-crop production completely.

The amount and importance of purchased necessities varies greatly from region to region and even from family to family. The particular qualities of the production regime are important for the degree of dependence on purchased necessities, as is the evolving cultural definition of necessity. Where the supply of hoes, seed, and cloth has failed, as in Mozambique, the effect on production has been disastrous. In much of rural Africa, lighting with kerosene, listening to the radio, using galvanized iron roofing, and consuming sugar have become the cultural norm; they are difficult to give up. The extent and quality of dependence on purchased goods varies a great deal, with implications that will be discussed below under 'reproduction'.

Prestige goods. African communities often give a special value to certain categories of goods, much as market societies value gold, diamonds, and perfume. Cattle in many places are kept as signs of wealth and status, as well as forms of savings. Cloth, iron bars, carvings, and many other things have circulated in special circuits of gift exchange. Sometimes prestige goods are part of the exchanges made to cement and celebrate a marriage. The cash market, which allows and encourages the creation of exchange equivalences among all goods has eroded the distinctiveness of prestige goods throughout Africa. Yet the special meaning of certain goods is reflected in the high cash price they fetch or in the reluctance of people to market cattle, for example, in a way that maximizes their cash income.

Where a prestige item such as cattle still has social recognition, possession of cattle becomes a source of social power and standing. Often the prestige item is tied to marriage exchanges and is used by elders as a way of controlling the achievement of social and economic independence by young people. This control does not insulate symbolic goods from the market; it can drive their price very high. As a result, young people may be forced into even greater dependence on wage labour or cash-crop production in order to attain full adult status in their own cultural terms (Meillassoux 1977), Stichter 1985, 15).

Maintaining and changing production

Peasant-farming units and regional systems of peasant farming have adapted to basic changes over the past few generations. Many of them adjusted to the ending of precolonial forms of servitude (which had often been reinforced by the transatlantic slave trade). They have adopted cash-crop farming and wage-labour export. In many places they have shaped themselves to widespread primary education and more selective secondary education. And in most places they have adjusted to a large increase in population. To maintain peasant-farming units and peasant-farming systems under these changed conditions has required continual adjustment in the way children are raised and the way roles of men and women are defined. It has meant choosing the most appropriate techniques of production from among those known to the community, from its own traditions and from the advice and information of experts, travellers, and experimenters.

Frequently, if not universally, there is a clear desire on the part of members of production units and farming systems to maintain the way of life they know, even in the face of great adversity. Thus do communities displaced by drought to refugee camps or urban fringes make their way back to their home areas when rains return, and the possibility of restarting the cycle of reproduction is restored. However, the capacity to maintain the system is sometimes snapped. Changes in farming may weaken the ecological basis of production, or a small alteration in climate may push the ecosystem past a threshold of viability. More commonly, the farming system survives, but it is unable to absorb the whole of the population it creates. Some members of most families must migrate to other regions and settings. Sometimes the money they send home becomes essential income for the survival of the community as a whole or for particular peasant-farming units in the community.

The desire not to change, or to conserve some essential qualities of life, may be one of the potent motivators of change in peasant-farming communities. In order to preserve what is regarded as essential, peasant farmers will make many adaptations and will organize in new ways to defend themselves. Under the stress of adaptation peasant-farming units change in many ways. Most obvious and striking are changes in settlement pattern and size of units. In some places large rural settlements broke up once central colonial authority ended the need for military defense. In what is now southwestern Tanzania, stockaded villages, which dated at least from the Ngoni migrations of the 1840s and the warfare that followed, broke up into a landscape of scattered homesteads once the colonial order was consolidated (Knight 1974, 20). In other places scattered farms tended to collect together around transportation routes. In the forest zone of Cameroon communities which had been gathered in an irregular circular pattern have rearranged themselves to straggle out in a narrow line along the new roads (Geschiere 1982). As the dwelling pattern changed to reflect the new social and economic conditions, so did the size of peasant farming units. Most frequently they became smaller, as young people struck out on their own to gain direct access to the money economy, either through wage work or through cash-crop production (Swindell 1985, 80).

Changes in settlement pattern and population of households are easy to see, but other important changes are less obvious. The fact that women in many African societies had primary responsibility for the production of food crops and that men were usually socially dominant in the household and the rural community has meant that men have better access to wage work and cash-crop earnings than do women. By and large women have remained in control of food production, in many cases taking on the work that men used to do, as men left to work elsewhere or spent more and more time on cash crops.

Although the patterns of change are various, the social values and political culture of rural producers and rural communities have been deeply affected by the integration into markets and nations.

Three circuits. The nature of change in peasant farming is made clearer by distinguishing three circuits of economic activity. One, the domestic circuit, is production for local consumption. Another, the external circuit, is production with the land and labour of the unit for sale on external markets; earnings are used for the purchase of goods from outside the community and the payment of taxes and other fees to external agencies. A third is the labour export circuit, which creates and exports labour for work outside the community and the remittance home of some wages for spending on local or external markets.

The three circuits are closely related, most directly through the fact that they draw on the same pool of labour. The two farming circuits also may compete for use of the same land. It was noted above that cash purchases of goods imported to the community may be essential to the maintenance of the domestic circuit of production. In the same way, the domestic circuit may be a critical support for the creation of labour to export or employ in cash-crop work. And the interaction among the production circuits may easily change the balance of the ecological exchange.

Ecological balance. All agriculture depends upon the maintenance of an exchange with nature. Historically, the balance in many parts of Africa was achieved through a system of agriculture which allowed fields to lie fallow for many years, after three or four years of farming had depleted the available fertility. Shifting cultivation had the advantage of being labour-efficient, since fields returned to brush and trees could be prepared for cultivation by cutting and burning the brush, rather less work than ploughing or digging fields grown up to grass and sod. Several common changes in peasant farming can threaten the ecological balance. Growing crops for the market and a rising rural population press peasant farmers into more intensive forms of cultivation. They crop the same fields

The **ecological balance** can affect the productivity of land and labour and the kind of equipment required. At the limit it can make farming impossible.

The **domestic circuit** of local exchange and self-provisioning may cease to supply basic needs. In time of crisis it may expand to meet needs unmet in the market circuit, but this capacity can be lost as labour and skills are drawn to the market and wage labour circuits.

Peasant farmers farm the land, mainly with family labour, using simple equipment, providing directly for many of their needs, and selling some of their production.

The **market circuit** opens outlets for production and pulls land and labour from the other circuits. It creates new needs for production and consumption goods. It may put new ecological pressure on the land. Through debt land rights may be lost

The **wage labour circuit** pulls labour from farm work and from the rural community. It sometimes brings in money and skills with returned workers. It changes needs and attitudes.

Figure 2 How ecological balance and the domestic, market, and wage-labour circuits change peasant farming

more often and bring marginal land under the hoe. Fallow periods are reduced or abandoned. Tree cover is cut for fuel. New methods of cultivation, such as ploughing, may alter the structure of the soil and increase its vulnerability to erosion. The result, all too frequently, is a degradation of the ecosystem which reduces the productivity of labour and adds to the pressures on the farming unit's ability to survive (Timberlake 1985).

Because the three production circuits and the ecological balance are so closely interrelated, farming units can follow different strategies of survival and improvement (Figure 2). At one extreme, they can try to maintain maximum independence from cash markets for crops and labour, emphasizing the domestic circuit and reducing risks of being harmed by market failures. Such a strategy forgoes the possible gains from market sales and the discretionary spending which cash income makes possible. A second extreme strategy is to favour market production or wage labour export in order to maximize cash income and flexible spending. The issues involved in working out a strategy are moral ones as well as income and security-related ones. What happens to family relationships when members go away to work in cities or other regions for long periods? How are family values affected by leaning towards domestic autonomy or towards maximizing cash income? With what community groups and tendencies is the family allying in choosing its method of adaptation? Young and old, women and men, individual and individual are likely to have different views and interests on these questions. In the working out of answers, family politics and social-economic strategy shape each other.

Peasant farms do not exist in isolation. Units producing similar crops and facing similar problems often exist side by side in the same village and in the same agricultural zone. The formation and the evolution of peasant-farming zones is the topic of the next chapter.

§ 4 §

THE MAKING OF PEASANT-FARMING ZONES

With all the emphasis on change in Africa it may come as a surprise to learn that the major rural–economic zones established over the past one hundred years in Africa have been strikingly durable. Many of them have gone through hard times, and some have been severely weakened, but most of them continue to exist, a number continue to expand, and a few thrive. The great export crops of Africa have been cotton, cocoa, coffee, tea, palm oil, and groundnuts (Map 2). Other crops of some importance include sesame, tobacco, cashews, pineapple, and pyrethrum. Sugar, rubber, and sisal have usually been grown as plantation or estate crops, although they are sometimes cultivated by smallholding peasant farmers. Even where countries have more than one export crop, they have often been divided into monocrop-zones, although zones which produce two major cash crops do exist. Historically, European settler zones, plantation-agriculture zones, and labour-export zones were also distinct social regions, but the distinctiveness of these areas has tended to diminish in recent years as settlers have emigrated, as plantations have been replaced by smallholders and contract farmers, and as workers in labour reserves have found a cash crop to grow or lost the distant market for their labour. As a result more complex mixed-zones are more common than they used to be, but the mark of the old rural–economic zones is still apparent in rural Africa. Peasant farmers are part of the society in all the zones, even in those where they do not represent the dominant type of agricultural economic unit. What model or theory best captures the dynamic of change in the emergence and evolution of peasant farming in Africa is the subject of great controversy. Before considering some of the contending ideas, it will be useful to have some cases in mind and to review the broad pattern of rural social–economic zones in sub-Saharan Africa.

TWO PEASANT-FARMING ZONES

Peasant farmers in sub-Saharan Africa are not like the ones Marx described in his study of the rural social structure of mid-nineteenth-century France (Marx 1963, 124). Marx wrote of a rural society 'formed by simple addition of homologous magnitudes, much as potatoes in a sack form a sack of potatoes.' As the examples of peasant-farming units show, the external relations of the units are very important to their functioning: labour, inputs, and marketing facilities are part of their everyday lives. Their access to land, labour, and loans is shaped by their place in the rural social and economic order. Many peasant farmers have off-farm work, as carpenters, masons, smiths, healers, traders, imams, and wage workers. And these professions, as well as many others, are part of community life. The state is also part of the local community in the form of local officials: village chiefs and subdistrict officers; agricultural extension agents and medical officers; police officers and teachers. The variety in the way different communities are structured, divided, united, and organized is very great indeed, as the following two examples begin to demonstrate.

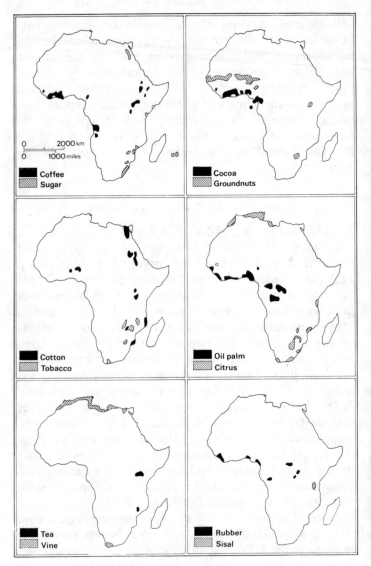

Map 2 Commercial Crops in Africa
Based on Griffiths, *An Atlas of African Affairs;*
London: Methuen, 1984. p. 121

Tanzania's southwestern coffee zone

There are several different ways to identify the zone around Mbozi District in the Mbeya Region of Tanzania. The administrative structures are themselves of great importance, but so are the cultural, economic, and environmental characteristics. The dominant ethnic group is the Nyiha who speak their own language. Many of them have been influenced by the Moravian Christian missions which established themselves in the area at the turn of the century and introduced coffee to the region. Coffee has also put a stamp on the zone. It was the crop that allowed a few dozen settler farms to survive, if not to flourish, during the interwar years and into the independence period up until the 1970s. The coffee estates attracted 1800 workers in 1938, most of them from the neighbouring Nyakyusa ethnic group. During the late 1930s Africa peasant-farming production of coffee also became established, with 551 growers producing 51 tons of coffee in 1940, the pre-war peak.

One of the permanent consequences of the coffee economy has been the creation of a multi-ethnic society in the region. The influx of non-Nyiha to the area was a source of concern to the British colonial authorities in the 1940s. They feared that the legitimacy of the Native Authorities would be undermined by the presence of 'alien natives' lacking the cement of tribal loyalty. Although an ordinance was passed giving chiefs the power to restrict entry from outside the district, it seems to have had little effect. By 1970 about 30 per cent of the population in ten randomly selected enumeration areas were non-Nyiha with the proportion of Nyiha ranging from a high of 100 per cent to a low of 40 per cent. The immigrant ethnic groups were mainly Ndali, Nyakyusa, and Lambia. They are now a settled and durable feature of the social landscape.

Coffee production also brought more intimate changes within production units themselves, affecting the relations among their members, as the farming unit described in chapter three demonstrated. A study carried out in 1967 which asked farmers to recall when they started growing coffee revealed a very rapid expansion from 1945 to 1967 (Knight 1974, 146). A socio-economic survey taken in 1970 which sampled farmers in ten census areas of the coffee growing zone of Unyiha division found that 80 per cent of the farming units grew coffee with an average of 2.1 acres per unit. Figures for 1970 show that farmers put great care into coffee production: 90 per cent weeded two times or more; 74 per cent used manure or mulch; 56 per cent used insecticides; 48 per cent used chemical fertilizers; and 40 per cent used fungicides (Jespersen 1971). These figures as well as qualitative research show that the adoption of coffee production has brought profound changes. Since the crop does not produce for the first three or four years, planting takes forethought and investment. Seedlings must be purchased or raised, transplanted, and protected from the sun. The labour and land expended on coffee requires changes in the organization of food-crop production. In the early years it was necessary to overcome opposition from the European settlers who strove to preserve their monopoly on coffee production and also from neighbours who resented the new crop and the changes it represented.

The influx of settlers, the creation of coffee fields by existing producers, and the assignment of land to Europeans began to put some pressure on land resources. The effect on production methods has been thoroughly documented (Knight 1974; Jespersen 1971). Within the Nyiha repertoire of cultivation techniques, there were two different strategies: first, land-extensive methods appropriate to woodlands requiring long fallow periods and the frequent shifting of cultivation to newly cleared fields; and second, more land-intensive methods appropriate to grasslands requiring shorter fallow periods. Within both systems the fallow periods could be shortened and the crop rotations altered. The trend in Unyiha has been from woodland to grassland systems and from long fallow to short fallow. New techniques and crops were brought by some of the immigrating peoples, including the Europeans. The intensification by the 1970s had gone furthest in the central-plateau part of the region where coffee cultivation and immigration were concentrated. There was some evidence of people who wanted to preserve the old ways moving to the fringes where there still was enough land for long fallow methods, but where it was not convenient to grow coffee. It should be noted, however, that there was no evidence in the 1970s that food production in the coffee areas had dropped. Even the coffee growers seemed to want to maintain their relative self-sufficiency in food.

Along with coffee was another carrier of the cash economy. People from Unyiha were drawn into wage employment in the nearby Lupa Gold fields, in the mines of southern Africa, and in the sisal estates in coastal Tanganyika. In the 1950s the colonial government, worried about the social effects of labour out-migration, commissioned a study. It found that one-fourth of the adult men and one-third of the young men were away working or seeking work. The main motive was economic, especially for young men wishing to earn money that would enable them to marry and set up their own households when they returned. In the richer coffee areas the rate of migration was lower. The study found that migration reflected intergenerational tension between elders and youth, but that the effects on the economy were not deleterious. It did not investigate the effects of migration or coffee production on the organization of labour and the social relations within family production units.

Labour migration later ceased to be a major issue. One by one the distant labour markets declined: first the gold in the Lupa fields gave out in the 1940s, then after 1963 the independent government discouraged migration to the mines, and finally the sisal estates became moribund in the face of competition from petroleum-based synthetic fibres. Still, wage labour shaped the experience of many men in the region and made it easier for men to hire on with the construction crews of the pipeline, the railroad, and the road which were built through the region to connect the Zambian copperbelt with the port of Dar es Salaam. Wage labour became a familiar and accepted part of the local economy.

Two other points need to be mentioned here. The first is that the social and economic changes already described were accompanied by growing, but limited, inequality of income among the farming population. In 1971 the evidence was that about 20 per cent of the farming units stood out as large producers, but less than one quarter of these acknowledged that they hired labour. Another 20 per cent were clearly small producers, distinctly poorer than the average and growing little or no coffee. The other 60 per cent grew both food and coffee and did not hire labour. In comparison to some other regions in 1972, Unyiha stood out for its continued use of cooperative labour.

Finally, the economic changes brought with them political changes. The social division between Christians and non-Christians remained significant, but the most prominent political organizations were the cooperative societies, which organized the marketing of coffee, and TANU (the Tanganyika African National Union), which rapidly established itself as the dominant nationalist party in the country during the 1950s. For a fleeting moment the local settlers tried to promote themselves as the rightful heirs to colonial power, if not as part of Tanganyika then by attaching the district to Zambia (then known as Northern Rhodesia), where settler power seemed briefly to have a future. Two more enduring conflicts have centred around the position of chiefs (promoted and tainted by the colonial system, but retaining some base in the local culture) and the relative influence of Nyakyusa and Nyiha interests and leaders in party and cooperative organizations.

The information needed to bring an account of Unyiha up to date is not readily available. Like most of rural Tanzania, people there were obliged to move into clustered villages in the mid 1970s. How this change has affected the economy, political organization, and local values and attitudes would be most interesting to know.

Senegal's groundnut zone

Senegal's peanut zone took recognizable shape around the turn of the century. The part of it of direct concern here, the region of Saloum (the name of a river and of a precolonial kingdom), gained its basic social structure very rapidly after 1910 when the construction of the Dakar–Niger railroad opened the area on a large scale to the groundnut trade and to settlement by immigrants from less fertile land further north. As in the case of the coffee zone of Unyiha, a new commercial crop, colonial rule, and religious innovation profoundly changed the population mix, the social stratification, the organization of production units, and the pattern of authority in the region of Saloum.

For several centuries before 1860 Saloum was a frontier state on the south-eastern edge of the Senegambian state system. Although it was one of a pair of kingdoms identified with the Serer ethnic group, Saloum in the 19th century and probably long before was culturally heterogeneous with many Tukulor, Fulani, and Wolof villages.

Well before the Islamic revolution which rocked the region after 1860, Muslim teachers, traders, and scribes had an active influence. And long before the French military conquest of 1887, European trade connections with establishments on the Gambia river and Cabo Verde were part of the social fabric (Klein 1968, 138).

The regional structure which now exists emerged only after a generation of turmoil and three-sided warfare. Muslim revolutionaries fought to conquer the older non-Muslim ruling houses and their supporters. The French imperialists with their armies and their trading companies embarked on their own policy of conquest, taking advantage of local conflicts. In Saloum they supported the more pliant royal claimants against the Muslims, defeating them in 1887. When the turmoil ended, the French had seized state power through military victory, Islam was an influential and growing movement which did not claim political power, and the old ruling families remained socially influential while accepting Islam and maintaining their presence in the new colonial administrative system (Klein 1968, 196).

Three partially distinct systems of social stratification were mingled in a single social order in the new groundnut economy. The old Saloum society of Serer, Wolof, Tukolor, and Fulani shared similar social distinctions among royalty; free agriculturalists and herders; endogamous specialists in trades (smiths, wood workers, musicians, leather workers, weavers, and potters); and dependants or slaves attached to families of the other groups. Dependants of agriculturalists were also agriculturalists. Some of the slaves of royalty were warriors, a group that expanded greatly during the period of warfare. Recent estimates suggest that together the slaves and the endogamous castes, which were also seen as socially inferior by the free groups, made up as much as 50 per cent of the population.

In old Saloum the different social ranks were closely associated in day-to-day village life. Each village (comprising several dozen extended-family units) or each small group of villages was relatively autonomous and self-sufficient in production. Caste lineages within a village or group of villages produced the tools, cloth, pots, clothing, and furniture used by the other households. All households, except perhaps for royalty in their special villages, worked at food production. A great part of the agricultural work was done by women. Fields close to the village were planted to early ripening millet, those further away were used for ordinary millet, and clay soil was appropriate for sorghum. Each family had a field of cotton, and also, from the 17th century when the American crops were adopted, a few plots of manioc and groundnuts for household consumption (Pelissier 1966, 155).

Islam evolved a second kind of stratification. Although the religion recognizes no essential hierarchy among the faithful in human dignity, the influential Muslim orders of Senegal – the Mouride and the Tijaniyya – created a distinction between the great maraboutic families of recognized religious leaders, and the ordinary adherents who give obedience and tithes to the latter. The distinction is given force in agriculture in the pioneer villages established by the Mourides in newly-settled lands. The marabout or his representative commanded the labour of a group of young men who worked under the direction of the leader and contributed the fruits of their labour to the order, which in turn saw to it that the disciples had their basic material needs met. The rigid control usually dissipated after the young men married and had families to support and administer, but the high standing of the marabouts and the founding families remains (Cruise O'Brien 1971, 163ff).

A third type of stratification evolved in direct association with the spread of groundnuts. Until 1964, peasant farmers got rights to land from original settlers or land chiefs in each locality, or from royal families to whom certain tracts had been allocated by a king. The right to farm the land was inherited within the farming families. Many families had a claim on more land than they could farm. With the advent of groundnuts many farmers contracted with seasonal immigrants allowing them seasonal farming rights to a plot of land in return for two or three days' work per week on the farmers' land. The immigrant farmers were called *navetanes* as a social category. Within the family-farming structure they took the position of *surga* or dependent farmer. Another kind of immigrant came only during the harvest season in the form of short-term labourers helping with the heavy work of pulling or digging the groundnuts and removing them from the plants (David 1980).

Less clearly in a subordinate relationship were the many immigrants from as far away as the Upper Volta who stayed in the region, some seeking permission to settle as organized villages and others settling as single families or as individuals marrying into the local society. Many of the latter were *navetanes* who decided to stay on. Other immigrants came not as farmers but as traders or craft specialists. Healers and hairdressers, water carriers and cloth sellers, Lebanese traders and French merchants found their way to the new trading towns and set up permanent or seasonal shops.

The result was a regional society with multiple hierarchies of dignity and of economic and social dependency. Social change and mixing opened opportunities for mobility and redefinitions of social standing. The dismantling of the ranks of warriors fed into the growing groundnut empire of the Muslim societies. The abolition of slavery and of restrictions on the castes opened the way for new careers in business and administration. Yet the sense of social hierarchy remains strong and its social and economic effects continue. The multiple and sometimes cross-cutting lines of subordination and superordination are the raw material with which builders of political factions and coalitions work. The party politics of decolonization built on these ties and divisions and resulted in the construction of a strongly dominant party with some legal and active opposition outside the party and much factional activity inside the dominant party. The resulting politics is intricate and time-consuming. It tends to conserve existing social inequalities and, partly for that reason, is also strikingly stable.

The central pillars of the colonial regional political economy were the administrative apparatus of the colonial state and the trade network of the colonial trading houses. Since Senegal's independence in 1960, both have been reformed, but trade power and administrative power remain in the armatures around which revolve the recurring relationships of the political economy. The administration has been enlarged and given a stronger orientation toward development. The all-important groundnut commerce was nationalized in 1964 and channelled through marketing cooperatives and a government marketing agency (Schumacher 1975). It became the financial base which nourished the elaborate factional constructions and conflicts of the dominant one-party system of political support for the government. In 1980 significant reforms fueled by scandals of embezzlement and pushed by international loan requirements returned much of the marketing chain to the private sector (Caswell 1984).

THE ORIGINS OF THE PEASANT-FARMING ZONES

The colonial partition of Africa left the imperial powers with the problem of making their conquest and subordination of the continent pay off, or at least pay for itself. The two cases are particular examples of solutions to that problem. Colonial governments needed an economic solution that would not trouble political order, or at least one that could be enforced at tolerable cost. The goals were not easily made compatible; to wring a surplus from the rural economy tended to change it in ways that threatened to disrupt public order. The four broad solutions they found for the problem helped to shape the enduring regional political economies of Africa. The solution which became dominant in West Africa and Uganda and in regions of many other colonies was the production of export crops by peasant farmers. Senegal's groundnut zone is an example. In this system African smallholders first added an export crop to their production repertoire. The export earnings could be taxed for state revenue and they generated import trade and internal trade which gave business to import–export firms. For peasant farmers the initial inducements to export agriculture were both positive and negative. Where cash income could not be assured or where its lure was not a sufficient incentive, colonial governments enforced cash tax payments or directly commanded each family to plant and to sell a certain amount of a cash crop.

In Kenya and Rhodesia, and in parts of Côte d'Ivoire, Tanzania, Zambia, Angola, Mozambique, and Zaire the task of generating new economic activity was placed in the hands of European immigrants who were given land on favourable terms as well as many other kinds of assistance to establish viable farms, sometimes very large ones. Africans found their place in the system as labourers and 'squatters' (farm workers allowed to live and grow food on the land of a European settler), and as displaced peasant farmers. With independence, as the case of south-western Tanzania exemplifies, peasant farming generally replaced colonial-settler farming.

A third pattern of agricultural organization was the plantation system. A transnational firm would be given the right to control land and to hire labour for large-scale production of an export crop. Very often the crop was one requiring local processing either to reduce bulk (as with sugar cane, oil palm, sisal, and rubber) or to maintain high quality (as with tea and arabica coffee). The large firm would gain the economies of scale in processing and exercise complete control over production. Nowhere in Africa are plantations the dominant form of agricultural organization, but there remain important plantations in Liberia (Firestone, for rubber), Zaire (Unilever, for oil palm), Mozambique (Sena Sugar Estates), Kenya (Brooke Bond, for tea), Cameroon (Unilever for oil palm), Tanzania (Brooke Bond for tea) and elsewhere. Some plantations have been nationalized (sisal in Tanzania) and some have withdrawn. Several companies have adopted outgrower or contract farming schemes (tea and sugar in Kenya, rubber in Côte d'Ivoire) as a way of expanding. A few colonial-style plantations remain, but more frequent now are state farms, joint government and private agri-industrial enterprises, and other centrally managed schemes which in many ways resemble plantations. Like plantations they have professional management, use machinery and other technology, and employ wage labour (Dinham and Hines 1983; Halfani and Barker 1984).

Many parts of Africa were subjected neither to smallholder cash-crop development, nor to the settler-farmer system, nor to plantations. Most of those were explicitly organized as labour reserves with agencies for recruiting and transporting workers (southern Mozambique is described later). Some, however, more spontaneously became labour-exporting regions as rural families under the compulsion of market pressures sent members to cash-earning jobs in mines, plantations, settler estates, industry, and urban trade and services, or to cash-farming regions as rural workers, labour tenants, or sharecroppers.

The crude division which had West Africa as the peasant farming zone, East Africa as the settler zone, and Southern Africa as the labour reserve zone for mines is only a crude approximation to reality. In fact most colonies had multiple types of rural zones. However, their smaller zones still often conform to the original types or to combinations of them (Amin 1976, 318).

Major peasant-farming zones

Having a dominant cash crop enforced upon farming communities a common calendar of farming activities, a shared dependence on a marketing and transportation system, and a similar relationship to the government's technical services and tax-collecting apparatus. A dominant cash crop proved to be a powerful structuring force affecting such basic relationships as land ownership, patterns of labour recruitment and control, settlement pattern, local political leadership, economic stratification, and focus of state power.

Cocoa in Ghana. Cocoa has been the mainstay of Ghana's economy since the early 1900s, although palm oil preceded cocoa as a commercial crop. In the mid 1800s peasant farmers of several different ethnic groups bought land from chiefs in the forest zone in eastern Akim and northern Akwapim on which to grow oil palm for export. This was one of the earliest examples of a peasant-farmer pioneer zone in Africa. Many others came into being in many parts of the continent in the century that followed. In Ghana the experience of commercial production of palm oil smoothed the way for the expansion of cocoa in the period after 1890. Cocoa, too, started with pioneer farmers buying land from chiefs and clearing parcels for the planting of trees. Land thereby entered the market, land ownership became more individualized, and new ethnically-mixed communities were created.

Existing social and economic relationships were adapted to meet the new situation. The sale of land, which conflicted with the accepted norm of residual lineage ownership of land, was based upon old rules that allowed the occasional transfer of parcels to refugees, exiles, and traders from outside the community. Groups of pioneer farmers were formed on the basis of customary lineage ties and customary non-kin associations, but they were used for the novel purpose of collecting the capital and the labour power to found a cocoa-growing settlement. New opportunities for the large numbers of social dependants, former slaves, and persons subject to debt-bondage loosened some of the old ties of personal dependence. However, it was the chiefs, traders, and people with personal dependants who could most rapidly found large cocoa farms, giving a new economic underpinning to old inequalities (Hill 1963).

In the early stages colonial officials favoured the expansion of markets, especially the market in land, and the destruction of the institutional power of chiefs. By 1912, however, the British colonial authorities were worried about the erosion of the old laws, customs, and practices which regulated social and economic life in rural Ghana. The challenge, as seen by the West African Land Committee established in 1912 to examine the question, was to restore food self-sufficiency, to stem the tide of land alienation, and to stop the emergence of a landless rural proletariat which threatened the law and order of customary institutions.

It became the project of the colonial state to foster and defend peasant farming by upholding what it understood to be customary land law: inalienability of basic lineage ownership; the right of community members to clear and use unallocated land and to pass on use-rights via rules of inheritance; and the power of chiefly institutions to regulate land allocation. In Ashanti, for example, where much of the later cocoa expansion took place, chiefs were encouraged to rent land to outsider farmers, but the sale of land was prohibited. Outsider farmers still entered to rent land. And, mainly from the drier regions further north still without major cash crops, came tens of thousands of *abusa* and *abune* sharecroppers (who receive one-third and one-half, respectively, of the cocoa they harvest). Other sharecroppers were drawn from the descendants of slaves and from indebted farmers.

Ghana's cocoa zone took on a political and social as well as an economic form, one containing tensions and conflicts. As more unoccupied land was planted to cocoa, the periods of bush fallow for food-crop holdings were reduced in length and food production suffered. Chiefs were able to manipulate their control of lineage lands to their own advantage, but younger farmers without aristocratic ties and with grievances began to organize drives to remove chiefs. Especially active against the aristocratic faction was the new group of relatively successful and ambitious medium- to large-scale farmers, farmer-traders, small merchants, school teachers, and clerks. Cocoa growers often found themselves in conflict with the trading companies over the price of cocoa and the price and supply of purchased goods. Farmers, as a result, several times organized collectively to refuse to sell their crops. The most powerful of these 'hold-ups', as they were called, took place in 1917–18, 1930–31 and 1937–39. The marketing board established in 1939 was meant to stabilize prices and to protect peasant farmers from damaging price swings. How it worked will be addressed in chapter five.

The colonial state tried to control the social pressures by preserving peasant-farmer production, and by strengthening the institution of chiefship and giving councils of chiefs more power at the provincial and territorial level. But the gravity of the tensions brought about by the commodity price-bust of the great depression brought the political economy of the cocoa zone into a generalized crisis. Low producer prices generated huge debt levels. Moreover, in the older cocoa areas it became difficult around 1930 to find any new land for cocoa, and ageing trees and swollen shoot disease began to reduce production. Emigration to new areas in Ashanti, Brong Ahafo, and elsewhere was discouraged by the restriction against land sales. The combined pressures in the region created a new export: young men with some schooling left in large numbers to seek a livelihood in the burgeoning cities of Accra, Kumasi, and Sekondi-Takoradi (Grier 1987). How the tensions in the cocoa zone energized the political conflicts of post-war Ghana will be discussed in chapter 7.

Cotton in Tanzania. One of Africa's great cotton farming regions is located south of Lake Victoria in Tanzania in five districts often referred to collectively as Sukumaland, after the ethnic group predominant in the area. The Sukuma people, now numbering more than 1.5 million, first adopted cotton production for sale with the encouragement, and sometimes the compulsion, of the German administrator of the region in 1910–1916 (Iliffe 1969, 169). Expansion of the export crop was given further impulse after Britain took control of the country, when the rail line from Tabora reached Mwanza on Lake Victoria in the late 1920s. Production rose steadily from under 3,000 bales in 1922 to 25,000 bales in 1948 when one of the most concerted regional rural development projects of post-war colonial Africa was initiated in Sukumaland. Thereafter production climbed rapidly. It reached 100,000 bales in 1955; 235,000 in 1963; and 350,000 in 1970 (Maguire 1969, 5 and 81; Tanzania 1972, 75).

The methods of cultivating cotton were very similar to those used for the staple food crops of sorghum and millet, and for maize, which replaced them in the late 1950s and early 1960s. However, the adoption of commercial production, and the new administrative system devised to promote planned agricultural development made a profound impact upon the peasant-farming society.

In the fifty-two Sukuma chiefdoms, each married male, and his family through him, had a right to a farm holding. Unmarried men had rights to single fields only. A married man could inherit an entire holding from his father or he could apply to the appropriate community leaders for a holding. In the case of uncleared land, the applicant needed only to inform the community authorities that he was creating a holding. Except for inheritance from father to son and limited lending of fields to relatives, the land holder had no right to dispose directly of his holding. It had to be reassigned by the community authority. As long as the land was farmed, farming practices were entirely a matter for the farm holder to decide. Although farming was the mainstay of the Sukuma economy, cattle were the main repository of wealth for prestige and security. They also served as a medium for large payments, such as bridewealth.

The Sukumaland Development Scheme which the colonial government put into effect in the 1950s attempted to enforce a wholly different kind of rationality on the expansion of cotton production which was taking place. It established a new hierarchy of councils and a set of administrative rules governing the allocation and use of land for farming and grazing, with the core intention of enforcing human and cattle densities determined by central colonial officials. Attempting to make the influx controls more palatable, the colonial officers contrived to have the native authorities enact them. The effect was to bring the native authorities under attack.

By 1953 or 1954 the Sukuma peasant felt that he was being pushed around. The tribulations of the present, not administrative-sponsored visions of the future, interested him most. Everywhere new rules, regulations and taxes seemed to require this, prohibit that, or take a few more shillings yearly from his pocket. He had to tie-ridge and manure certain portions of his fields, plant specified minimum acreages of cassava (as an antifamine measure) and cotton, plant at certain times and pull out cotton stalks by certain dates for burning after harvest, refrain from cultivating near gullies, cutting trees, or transporting cattle without a permit, have his cattle dipped or innoculated against disease, slaughter or sell a certain percentage of his cattle each year and produce on request certificates indicating sale or attesting that the hides from slaughtered beasts had been seen by the appropriate government officer.

(Maguire 1969, 31–32)

Colonial policy supported the establishment of Asian traders as the intermediaries between the cotton growers and the external market. Resentment of their trading practices sparked a move by African traders and farmers to create marketing cooperatives. Colonial researchers and administrators believed that the rapid spread of cotton production and population increase were intensifying cultivation and grazing to the point where ecological balance was gravely threatened. The stringent rules about settlement, cultivation, and grazing which the government tried to enforce clashed profoundly with customary institutions of land holding. The resulting discontent helped to fuel support in the 1950s for the Tanganyika African National Union and its drive for independence, a topic which will be addressed in chapter 7.

Peasant farming and large-scale agriculture

Large-scale agriculture, whether in the form of settler farms – which were often of modest size by plantation standards – or large plantations, did not supplant peasant farming. By taking land away from existing or potential peasant farmers it limited their expansion and pressed them to more intensive, and often more destructive, use of the land. Since settler farms and plantations sold crops and hired labour, their owners and managers had an interest both in preventing African peasant farmers from selling market crops and in obliging them to sell their labour cheaply. Settler and plantation interests were often successful in having colonial governments restrict African commercial farming, while imposing hut taxes and head taxes along with labour obligations to induce Africans to work at low wages.

In the case of colonial Kenya such policies prevented Africans in Central Province from growing high-value export crops like coffee in the 1930s and 1940s and forced them to become labourers and squatters on European holdings. Some African farmers were able to turn the more intensive farming necessary on their restricted holdings to some benefit. Making use of the knowledge about crops and techniques they learned while working on the European estates, African farmers expanded their production of tea, pyrethrum, livestock, milk, and marketable food crops. However, these advances could not offset the new pressures on peasant farming brought by the colonial policy of the 1950s. The British promoted closer settlement and more intensive production on the 20 per cent of the agricultural land which was in settler hands. The African 'squatters' who had been allowed to live on the European estates and to grow food and graze livestock there in partial payment for their labour were forced to return to the African farming areas which were already overcrowded and in which they often had no operational rights to land. The consequent tensions and resentments contributed to the Mau Mau revolt and the formation of the Land Freedom Army. The colonial response combined stiff repression with the promotion of a peasant-farming elite enjoying individual land ownership. The stage was set for the politics of decolonization and the expansion of a peasant-farming sector – one with marked inequalities – at the expense of the settler estates (Heyer 1981, 95–101).

Another example of adaptability of peasant farming, this time to the requirements of large-scale long-distance labour migration, is given below.

DIFFERENT KINDS OF PEASANT-FARMING ZONE

The examples of different sorts of peasant farming in sub-Saharan Africa make two points clear: first, that peasant farming does vary in extremely significant ways which affect economic and political dynamics and, second, that community-wide and region-wide patterns of incorporation of peasant-farming units are essential to understanding how peasant farming works. An account of some strikingly different types of peasant-farming zones will begin to demonstrate the kinds of differences in peasant farming that are interesting.

Annual crops and perennial crops

Labour, not land, has historically been the major constraint on production. Within the cash-crop category there are important differences in labour needs between those zones that specialize in annual crops (cotton, peanuts, and sesame for cash; millets and sorghums for food) and occupy the drier savanna regions that make up the majority of the land area of the continental region, and those that specialize in perennial tree crops (coffee, tea, and cocoa for cash; yams and bananas for food) and occupy the wetter coastal and mountain zones of the continent (Tosh 1980).

In the drier grain-growing zones the quantity and distribution of rainfall varies a great deal from year to year. Crop failures are frequent. Fields have to be planted each year, which requires preparing the fields and careful weeding. Moreover, agricultural work must be crowded into a growing season of only four to seven months, and the annual crops are more demanding of labour. Since planting and weeding are dictated by the onset of the rains, food crops and cash crops compete with each other quite directly for labour. There are pronounced periods of high labour demand when cash crops and food crops compete for attention. The most critical are planting, when the rains begin, and weeding, early in the growing season. Getting advantage of the early days of moisture can make a big difference in the yield of a crop. Families have to decide whether to give that advantage to cotton or to millet.

In the days before commercial agriculture the need to prepare fields in time for the rains and to plant as soon as the rains began was met by cooperative work groups of many different forms. Women, youth, relatives, and villagers would form up a team to prepare the fields, or to plant or harvest the crop of each member in turn. The farmer benefiting from the labour would, perhaps, supply a feast or beer for the work team. In more egalitarian societies the work was purely reciprocal, but in some more stratified societies the work was tantamount to paid labour by poorer farmers for richer ones. With commercialization and growing inequality, cooperative work groups, especially in the stratified societies, became more like wage labour or died away in favour of other forms of labour-transfer from poor to rich.

In the wetter tree-crop zones the seasonal work pressure is less intense. Food and cash crops tend to follow different schedules and often they can be interplanted, minimizing the competition for labour. In addition, the division of labour between men and women tended to be different in the two zones. In the savanna men did a great deal of agricultural work, concentrating on the clearing and preparing of fields while women did most of the planting and weeding; men and women shared the work of harvesting. In the forest zones men often did little agricultural work at all, or else tended special crops like yams. They could take on the work of establishing cash crops. Although clearing forest land for fields is hard work, once coffee, cocoa, or plantains are established the work is spread more evenly through the year. Often the period of heavy labour on the cash crop, such as harvesting, occurs when there is little work to do on the food crops. The commitment of male labour to cash crops had a much smaller effect on food crop production in the forest zones than it did in the savanna areas. As a consequence the social dynamics of cash-crop production are quite different in the two zones.

Each cash crop has its own requirements. Of the savanna crops, cotton is the most demanding of careful labour, peanuts are next, and sesame is least demanding. The European textile industry wanted inexpensive cotton. The difficulty of growing rain-fed cotton and its competition with food crops explains why it was the crop most often singled out for compulsory production by colonial governments and even by some of the postcolonial governments. Peanuts had another advantage besides being less demanding of labour; in a pinch the family could eat peanuts whereas cotton has very little use value. Of the forest or tree crops, tea requires the most disciplined attention.

Peasant-worker zones

Some of the dry grain-farming zones of African agriculture are integrated into the market through systematic export of wage labour, either instead of or in addition to growing crops for sale. Such regions are sometimes called labour reserves, but as farming regions they are peasant-worker zones or areas of wage-dependent agriculture. The fundamental point is that the maintenance of the agricultural system requires the continuation of wage labour. A large zone of wage-dependent agriculture developed in southern Mozambique as a result of the promotion of labour export to South Africa by the Portuguese colonial government. The withdrawal of male labour reduced the productivity and variety of the region's farming and made it dependent upon the injection of wages from returning miners. The degree to which agriculture itself depended on the wages and the goods imported by the mine workers became visible when South Africa restricted its labour imports, and a grave crisis in agriculture in southern Mozambique ensued (Bowen 1986).

With half the working-age men absent, changes in farming were inevitable. Millet and sorghum gave way to maize as the major food crop. Maize produced more grain per hour of labour under favourable conditions of moisture. The proper conditions could not be guaranteed in hoe cultivation on the uplands where millet and sorghum had been grown. The heavy clay soils of the river valleys kept their moisture and could support year-round cultivation, but they had to be ploughed with oxen. More and more land came under the plough. Although women took a growing share of the farm work, the ploughing was usually done by men with ox teams hired for the purpose. The money to pay for the ploughing and the maize seed came from mining wages. Mining wages also helped families through the years when the rivers flooded and destroyed the lowland maize crop (Young 1977).

A few richer farmers broke out of the labour migration cycle. Encouraged by the colonial government, they hired more labour and began to grow food for the urban market. They might also have lent money or sold food to their less productive farming neighbours who remained dependent on mining wages. The restriction of mining employment, the flight of the Portuguese traders and technicians, and the experience of calamitous floods and droughts created a deep crisis in the region's agriculture by the late 1970s; a crisis which has only been deepened in the late 1980s by the attacks on government services and projects and on transport, by the South African-supplied Renamo guerrillas.

Other regions of wage-dependent agriculture characterized the dry-farming zones to the north of the forest agriculture in West Africa. Burkina Faso has large regions dependent on wages earned in Ghana and Côte d'Ivoire. The adoption of cash crops like cotton and peanuts in these savanna areas has corresponded with a relative decline in migrant labour.

Pioneer zones

As the earlier descriptions of cocoa farming in Ghana and groundnut farming in Senegal noted, peasant farming is often very rapidly established and quickly spread via the settlement of an area by people from outside. A new settlement may not mean that the land was empty or unclaimed. In the case of Senegal the pioneer villages, with the support of the colonial state, took land from pastoralists. In the case of Ghana pioneer cacao farmers bought forest land not under active use from the chiefs in the area. But the new settlements were established with their own rules and customs. They were freer to develop new practices than were established communites adapting to cash-crop agriculture. In Senegal the Mouride form of Islam and the idea of strict obedience to a religious authority first regulated many of the pioneer settlements. In Ghana the idea of capitalist production and forms of association brought from their home region guided the new communities.

In Tanzania field researchers have studied several pioneer peasant-farming zones growing such different crops as rice (Usangu), wheat (Arusha), and maize (Ismani). The pioneer zones have in common ethnic diversity, rough and tough social interaction, strongly emerging class relations, and a widespread acceptance of gaining wealth as a personal and community goal (Awiti 1975; Feldman 1971; Raikes 1975; Pipping 1976; Walsh 1985).

It is likely that by taking people out of their old context and away from old authorities it is easier to instil new values and practices. The social strains and tensions of pioneer settlements may also favour social and cultural innovation. Governments and other organizations have tried to make use of the innovative potential of pioneer zones in a wide variety of settlement schemes, but these take on quite a different character from the more spontaneous pioneer zones.

Planned settlements and state peasantries

Tanzania made the most extensive use of the principle of innovation by planned resettlement in its massive and much-criticized villagization policy in the mid 1970s. The new villages were very large and often represented a change fom scattered homesteads to clustered settlements with all the adjustment of social relations that close habitation requires. Tanzania's policy stands out, but Ethiopia has carried out an even larger programme of resettlement in villages, and many other governments have less massive policies of encouraging the relocation and clustering of peasant-farming settlements in order to improve government services and reduce transport and communications costs. Often there is also spontaneous resettlement along new roads and at the junctions of transportation routes. And most governments have at least a small policy of assisted resettlement schemes designed to establish better farming practices.

In planned schemes the government exercises a high degree of control. Membership is often at the discretion of the administrative agency. Crops, methods of cultivation, location and construction of dwellings, and other aspects of community life are more or less closely prescribed by the scheme management. On the whole the efforts to create state supervised peasantries have not succeeded as economically viable ways of achieving social and economic innovation. They are expensive and frequently they are not very productive (Hill 1977). Some examples of post-independence schemes will be noted in chapter 5 where efforts to gain greater control over production are discussed.

Intensive versus extensive farming

African agriculture tends to spread labour out over comparatively large areas of land. Peasant farmers in Asia pour many more hours of work into each hectare of land than do peasant farmers in Africa. The farming routine of intensive agriculture uses the same fields most years, allowing only short fallow periods. Since nutrients are steadily removed from the soil, it includes regular efforts to restore and improve the fertility by the application of animal and human waste and other organic material. The rationality of extensive agriculture under Africa's environmental conditions is now much better understood than it was early in the colonial era, when African farming practices were often dismissed as being haphazard and ineffective. Although the rationality of the long fallow or bush fallow agricultural systems is widely admitted for circumstances of low-population density, agronomists foresee a need to intensify production. They have identified a number of zones where intensive agriculture is already practised. In some cases it evolved recently while in others the system is an ancient one (Netting, Cleveland, and Stier 1980).

In Senegal, for example, the Serer ethnic group who farm in the same region as the Wolof have associated stock keeping with crop raising since before the colonial period. They pen their herds on their grain fields after the harvest and during fallow years in the normal, short rotation. Under increasing population pressure they have further intensified cultivation of land near their villages. To do this they have had to place their cattle far from the village, losing the opportunity to add manure to some of their regularly cultivated fields. They appear to have entered a process of 'agricultural involution' in which the return per hour of labour in agriculture decreases as the quantity of labour per unit of land increases. Worse still is that the environmental base of the agricultural system is degraded by the intensification process (Lericollais 1972).

A similar circle of cumulative causation is reported for the Kusasi of northern Ghana (Netting, Cleveland, and Stier 1980). The men tend and manure carefully the sorghum and millet field close to the compound, while women cultivate a kitchen garden. High and increasing population density and chronic hunger have driven them to intensify cultivation even further in recent years. Schemes to introduce new cash crops in the region have failed to give them a better return for their labour. Craft production, labour migration, and emigration are more attractive prospects than trying to grow cotton or rice. There is no apparent way to push intensification onto a track of increasing productivity of labour. In the Hausa region of northern Nigeria, on the other hand, there are examples of intensified dry-zone agriculture in the vicinity of historic cities that does give a reasonable return to the added labour, although most peasant farmers would prefer to combine intensive agriculture with part-time off-farm employment (Netting, Cleveland, and Stier 1980, 371).

From types of region to regional political economies

Of course the types noted above do not constitute a logically constructed and exhaustive typology linked to a theoretical apparatus. Rather they are a list of types, each designed *ad hoc* to clarify particular limited questions. They do suggest, however, that the key to grasping the dynamics of change in rural Africa and the connections between rural people (as citizens and producers) and the state is the idea of political–economic regions. The alternative approach of studying the relationship between state and individual production units is stymied by the huge variation in the structure and activity of production units and by their important connections with one another. The amount of off-farm work, the importance of pastoralism, the frequency of seasonal migration, and the variety of combinations of economic activity in rural Africa ensure that any simple notion of direct state–peasant relations will frequently mislead.

The idea of regional political economies has the great virtue of bringing together a view of the organization of production units with an account of the networks and connections which differentiate them. In particular it allows a clear look at the links between state and rural society which typically pass through regional intermediaries, whose positions and powers grow out of the regional political economy. The excellent studies from which the regional types listed above were drawn offer a start on the identification of types of regional political economies.

In order to move toward a meaningful analysis of regional political economies, we need a better grasp of the larger forces which shape regions and govern change within them. Chapter 5, which follows, describes a major force which both organizes rural regions and causes tensions within them: the market. Chapter 6 then examines the way tensions are generated within production units and communities. Chapters 7 and 8 return the analysis to the national political economy of peasant farming and focus again on the idea of regional political economies.

§ 5 §

MARKETS AND POWER

When peasant farmers market their crops, they participate in the division of profits along the chain of those who handle the crop (Table 6). Peasant farmers, local marketing agents, transporters, bulk marketers, shippers, processors, and retailers all assert the need to cover their costs. In the case of export crops, since the final price is set by the world market or by a trade agreement, there is no latitude in the total amount to be allocated. What one party gains another one loses; it is a classic zero-sum game. The colonial pattern was for the marketing companies to use their monopoly power to set prices against farmers who had little capacity to organize and who were often forbidden by law to unite against the buyers. However, in the period since independence it has become clear that the structure of the marketing relationship remains a source of conflict. It is a conflict, centred in economic allocation, which intimately involves the government. Post-colonial governments have used their control in marketing export crops as a mechanism for taxing lines of production, which are often important sources of foreign exchange and relatively reliable sources of revenue for the government treasury. Peasant farmers, of course, want a reasonable share of the value of the crops they produce and understandably object when the value they receive declines.

The detailed involvement of governments in the pricing

Table 6 The marketing chain and opportunities for income

Activity	Social group	Opportunity for gain
Growing crops for sale	Peasant farmers, capitalist farms, plantations.	Selling above cost of production. Pressure to keep costs low.
Transporting crop to market	Peasant farmers, traders, transporters who own trucks or wagons.	Reduce payment to others in case of peasant farmers doing own transport. Charging fee to transport for others.
Marketing crop	Private traders, cooperative marketing agencies, government buyers, some specialized workers to handle crop and to keep records.	Profit margin, fee paid by government for marketing service, opportunity to cheat. Wages, in case of workers.
Bulk transport of crop	Railroads and road transport companies both private and public. Private transporters often work under government licence.	Fee for service, use of rights to fuel for other transport.
Processing the crop	Producers do some local drying and treating of coffee, cocoa, tea, cotton. Private or state-owned industries do	Earnings often set by government within limits of world price levels. Earnings go to international business, national

Table 6 *(cont.)*

Activity	Social group	Opportunity for gain
	large-scale centralized processing of groundnuts, oil palm for export.	business, and government enterprise.
More processing, packaging, and retailing	Often takes place in developed countries. Frequently managed by multinational enterprises.	National and international private business.

and marketing of marketed crops, especially export crops, has brought about a particularly close relationship among states, marketing institutions, and peasant farmers. It should be stressed that the relationship of state to peasant farmer is not totally antagonistic. Peasant farmers (if they are to remain peasant farmers) need a government or a similar agency to establish and maintain marketing organizations, or the conditions which allow them to exist. States (at least for many years to come) need peasant farmers to continue to produce taxable and marketable crops. Both share an interest in high world prices and increased returns to land and to labour – a larger pie about whose allocation they will certainly conflict. Mutual dependence and conflict are both built into the relationship. For peasant producers the material core of the relationship is a continuing preoccupation. The marketing moment is the transaction in which they realize whatever gains their cash-crop work has earned. Marketing needs to be placed in a wider context, however. In this chapter attention will be given to the origins and evolution of marketing agencies, the relation of marketing to politics (organization, patronage, and leadership), the taxation of marketed exports, and the use of market power to shape production.

The market relationship is currently the subject of a lively debate which has direct and intended policy implications for African governments, for international financial institutions, and for peasant farmers and the organizations which purport to reflect their interests. A still influential position put forward by the World Bank in 1981 holds that the problems of agricultural development in Africa are essentially problems of interference in markets. If producer prices were allowed to reflect world market prices and if smoothly operating mechanisms for receiving and transporting crops and for making payments were established – so runs the argument – then the development problem would largely take care of itself. Get governments to stop distorting the market pattern and to establish the institutional requirements for the markets to work, and work they will (World Bank 1981).

The reasoning here assumes that peasant-farmer production of cash crops will respond to incentives of price and cost. Peasant farmers may engage in self-provisioning, but that fact has no major effect upon their market behaviour. As producers of marketed crops and purchasers of farm inputs as well as consumer goods, peasant farmers try to maximize their net purchasing power. The way to improve peasant farmer production is to get the prices right. We can call this the *market peasant* argument.

A second argument starts from the premise that the second leg of peasant farming, self-provisioning, can set the stride for positive change. The capacity of peasant farmers for self-reliant production, says the argument, is the key to a healthy agricultural economy. Self-provisioning has been systematically undermined by growing participation in market production. Once it is restored, expanded production of food can be assured and the production of export crops can be pursued. We can call this the *self-reliant peasant* argument (Timberlake 1985, 72–78).

A third view agrees that self-provisioning remains important, but holds that it is an obstacle to progressive economic change. It gives peasant farmers what is called an 'exit option', a viable choice to abandon market production. Self-provisioning lacks the potential for large gains in productivity while protecting peasant farmers from the full force of market relationships; the peasant farmers are not subject to the full discipline of the market and do not respond to the incentives to improve productivity. Only when they are fully captured by market forces will peasant farmers begin to implement their capacity to improve productivity of land and labour. We can call this the *uncaptured peasant* argument (Hyden 1980).

Each of the three arguments goes beyond the market relationship to discuss some of the political and social dimensions of peasant farmers' links to the state. These discussions will be pursued in chapters 7 and 8. The provisional conclusion is that both market responsiveness and self-provisioning may have either positive or negative consequences for improving agriculture. Which relationship holds depends on the way 'agricultural improvement' is defined (in terms of marketed output or meeting basic needs) and on circumstances such as the farm-gate price levels and the political strength of peasant farmers.

MARKETS AND PEASANT FARMERS

High drama is concentrated in the setting in which peasant farmers sell their crops. First the farmers have to harvest a crop, which often represents the fruit of their labour of an

entire growing season and their cash income for a whole
year. Then they have to process it, pack it up, and
transport it to a marketing point. Because coffee has high
value by weight and has good storage properties, growers
in Mbozi district (Tanzania) in 1972 could carry their
harvest down from the hills in 20 litre kerosene containers
on the backs of bicycles, load by load, over a period of
weeks. They delivered the coffee to a government buying
station in a permanent building which also served as a
warehouse for chemicals and sprayers to be sold to the
coffee farmers. In Senegal, a farming unit might pack its
entire peanut crop into a dozen or more burlap bags, load
them into a donkey cart, and haul them to a cooperative
consisting of a shade shelter, a scales, and a huge mound of
peanuts piled out of doors behind temporary fencing. That
is the way marketing was handled in Birkelane district in
Senegal. The money (or in some cases, promissory notes)
received in one transaction on one day in the year or in a
few transactions over a period of days or weeks often
represents the entire cash income of the productive unit.
Tea is one of the rare crops in which harvest and sale are
spread fairly evenly throughout the year. Cotton, cocoa,
and sesame concentrate the drama of the market
encounter into a short season when money circulates
rapidly for a short time in the rural economy before
flowing back to the cities and countries whence it came.

The disadvantage of the producers

In production peasant farmers usually have day-to-day
control over their work and their crop; in the marketing
relationship they are no longer in control. The buyers and
the government regulate the process. Inspectors may
examine the crop and grade it for quality. Before placing
bags of peanuts on the scale, the seller in full view of the
purchaser must pass them through a rotary sieve which

allows sand, dirt, and debris to fall out. The purchaser then weighs the peanuts, records their weight, and calculates the price; making deductions for quality defects, handling costs at the marketing station, and debts owed by the seller. For many crops sold to cooperatives there is a first payment at the moment of delivery and a second payment months later which reflects the price finally achieved on the world market, less marketing costs and other levies. There is often much opportunity for fraud: rigged scales, false prices, dishonest mathematics, and sales conditioned on later purchases. The producers, too, can try their hand at deception, for example by concealing stones in their crops to augment the weight. They may evade debts by having another person conduct the sale in his or her own name. In the contest of wits the producers are often at a great disadvantage, if only because they do not have the skills of literacy and numeracy to check the books and verify the receipts. In addition they usually face a single buyer or one of a few organized buyers, leaving the producers little choice about where and how to sell. It would be inaccurate to see the producers as totally helpless: producers have held up sales of their crops and have created alternative marketing channels, especially in border regions. But when the monopoly position of the buyers is combined with their skills in bookkeeping and their inevitably strong connections with state power and political influence, the structural disadvantage of the producers stands out.

The structural disadvantage of peasant farmers in the division of benefits is one reason that it has been rare for peasant farmers to become prosperous expanders of production. For ambitious and well-placed farmers, the road to prosperity and social standing has more often been one of diversifying (either as a private operator or as an activist in the cooperative movement) along the chain of marketing, supply, and transportation which links peasant farming to world markets. Rather than enlarging the farm, a successful peasant farmer will buy a small truck and enter the business of carrying crops to market. He or she may also become a purchasing agent for the crop and a retailer of consumption goods and farming inputs. It is easier to achieve wealth in trade and transport than in farming (Iliffe 1983, 23–43).

Locally successful merchants and transporters are important intermediaries linking their community to wider social and political structures. Very often their economic activity brings them into relation with the state. Transport, crop purchase, and retailing of basic commodities are frequently licensed by the state. The aspiring entrepreneur has first to seek government approval. Where marketing is assigned to cooperatives, government control is usually quite direct. By controlling marketing the state is also cementing its links with prominent and influential members of local communities. It is no wonder that expansive farmer–transporter–merchants are very often also local political leaders.

Community divisions and spatial patterns

Just as local agents for the marketing system emerge from the community of peasant farmers, so does the central administration of the marketing system send its agents into rural communities. These may be the officials of the marketing board or the professional staff provided to marketing cooperatives. Within the rural community, then, are three different kinds of participants in the marketing chain. Peasant farmers who sell crops; farmer-traders with roots in the community; and marketing system agents tied to the central marketing bodies and posted in the community. In addition the central marketing body itself maintains an interest in the way the system functions in the community. Within the locality the pulling and tugging over the division of proceeds is not a simple two-way struggle. All producers want higher prices; large producers want special benefits as producers and as marketers and transporters (and they often have the clout to get them); local agents want higher salaries and scope for profit-making; the central system wants to maximize its revenue. These conflicts tie into other divisions and stratifications in the rural community.

The spatial pattern of market towns and the physical layout of shops express the ambivalent presence of external agencies and the partial separation of local intermediaries within a rural community. Birkelane, in Senegal, for example, was built to be a market town (Barker 1987). A small village had occupied the site, but the town was founded when the railroad opened the area to groundnut farming. Colonial planners gathered the large European trading companies in a rectangle of large one-story buildings facing the market square, which they located strategically between the railroad and the main road. They had the principal residential area laid out on the other side of the tracks. They placed the office of the subdistrict administrative officer near the road carrying traffic from Dakar and Kaolack to eastern Senegal. The police station and the post office were built near the market square. The forces of the cash market and the administrative state ran powerfully through the market square. Each year, during the short season of very active peanut trading from January to March, the economic currents took material form in the large bundles of banknotes which exchanged hands at the peanut marketing points and soon found their way into the safes and pockets of the merchants and tax collectors around the market square. The market town of Vwawa in the coffee-growing region of southwestern Tanzania had a remarkably similar physiognomy.

The shops in the two towns were also of similar design. In Birkelane and Vwawa the typical shop of a merchant selling consumer goods like cloth and kerosene had a strongly marked boundary between the townspeople and the merchant. A high counter split the shop along its length giving a wide area for the would-be consumers to crowd up to see the merchandise, while simultaneously protecting the merchant and the goods from the potential buyers. In Birkelane merchants who purchased peanuts from peasant farmers had scales and storage areas behind or beside their shops. The peasant farmer could easily step into the shop to begin spending whatever cash he had received from the merchant after outstanding debts were deducted from the account.

Similar layout of market towns and similar design of retail shops all over the continent have built the circuits of trade and administration into the townscape and architecture of rural centres, giving them a palpable presence which sets them apart from the more domestic forms of social life. Of course the market places and administrative offices themselves attract and generate their own social relations. They become part of the community, too. Meetings and dances are also held in the market square of Birkelane, and the subtle interactions of patrons and clients and interest groups are knit across the shop counters and the office desks, in the shade of the large verandas, and in the cool, subdued light of back rooms. Two strong polarizing forces sustain and structure the more complex relations: the energy of the market and the power of the administration.

GOVERNMENTS AND EXPORT MARKETS

The effort mounted since 1981 by international financial interests, to induce governments in Africa to relax their grip on the market link to rural producers, is sometimes presented as a return to an original and natural condition in which trading and governing subsist in independent spheres. In fact long distance trade was so closely connected with political power and government revenue in several of the precolonial kingdoms of Africa that it has been proposed as a distinctive feature of a specific African mode of production (Coquery-Vidrovitch 1969). Moreover, many of Africa's colonial governments began as trading companies with a licence to exercise government functions. The imposition of specialized colonial governments set up a boundary between colonial administration and the large trading companies, but it was a boundary demarcating cooperative partnership rather than fierce antagonism. Colonial governments helped the trading companies by barring Africans from trading operations, creating monopolies or oligopolies with reduced competition, legislating for trading centres and contracts of sale, discouraging or outlawing producer cartels, requiring the delivery of certain crops, distributing seed, imposing personal and family taxes which required cash payments and therefore cash earnings, and facilitating the introduction of new cash crops. During the Second World War Britain had strong reason to extend control over marketing profits and the planning of crop production within its empire. It set up marketing boards to accomplish these tasks and claimed they would also be used to stabilize the prices to producers. In fact they began a process carried out with great energy by the successor governments in independent Africa. The marketing boards taxed the producers and fed hard currency to the government, in this case the British government (Hopkins 1973, 286–288; Beckman 1981, 145–146).

Independent governments carried on the intimate connection with export crop marketing. In West Africa the marketing boards were more inclined to tax producers than were the boards in East Africa which had at the outset to contend with the pressures and claims of European settler farmers for favourable prices. The affinity for control of export-crop marketing was driven by government need for revenue and for control over the economic transactions where taxation was administratively easy. Controlling the agency which served as intermediary between thousands of small producers and the large buyers on the world market was the optimum strategy. The government could then license private intermediaries between itself and the producers, or it could encourage the formation of a cooperative marketing system over which it could exercise closer or more distant control. Alternatively, the government could create its own crop authorities to carry out trade with the producers.

In the marketing of peasant farmers' crops was ample opportunity for patronage. Licences to buy, sell, or transport crops; jobs in marketing agencies and positions in cooperatives; loans: all these could be allocated in such a way as to build a following or cement a clientele. The favoured-few gained 'monopoly rents' (Bates 1981) from their favoured market positions and they got social privilege and political influence from their standing with government and dominant party. In some cases the patronage seems to have eased the relations among cultural communities; in others it seems to have exacerbated ethnic rivalries. Sometimes, as in the case of Nkrumah's Ghana, governments came to have tense and antagonistic relationships with precisely those rural regions with the strongest political organization and the most articulate rural-based leadership (Beckman 1976). Handling the politics of marketing often became a major preoccupation of internal politics.

There were also reasons in development planning for control of the major source of investment in the country

(Helleiner 1966). Cocoa earnings in Ghana, for example, were a genuine national resource and it is not obvious why cocoa growers should reap the entire windfall of rising world prices (nor why they should absorb the whole cost of diving world prices). Roads, schools, industries, and new crops might be financed out of the cocoa earnings to the benefit of many Ghanaians. In the days of high commodity prices which stimulated the expansion of production of cocoa, tea, coffee, cotton, and groundnuts in Africa in the 1950s and early 1960s, governments found they could pay the growers the usual price and still have income to spend on government services and development projects. Nkrumah's Seven Year Plan was the most striking case of a government attempting to use its agricultural earnings to industrialize and diversify the economy while covering over social conflicts with patronage and some repression (Genoud 1969). As the cocoa price slid downward the pressure to squeeze the income of cocoa producers mounted. Even after Nkrumah was overthrown in 1966 and a series of governments professing philosophies quite different from his achieved power, the squeezing of cocoa earnings continued with the ultimate effect of severely weakening production.

Cocoa output, which normally provided some 60 per cent of export earnings, plummeted from a high of 557,000 long tons in the 1964–65 crop year to 277,000 in 1977–78 and to an estimated 100,000 tons in 1983–84. Many different factors are responsible for this decline in production – the cutting out of cocoa trees in favour of food crops, ageing cocoa trees, bush fires, poor roads and lack of transport, low prices and lack of prompt payment, inadequate labour, ineffective control of pests and diseases, unavailability of inputs, inadequate storage facilities, smuggling, and a decline in the quality of extension services – making no simple solution possible for an incoming regime like Rawlings.

(Rothchild and Gyimah-Boadi 1986, 260)

Many other governments in Africa have followed the same pattern of maiming and frightening, if not killing, the geese that lay the golden eggs of agricultural exports.

Gaining control of production

Even as they taxed cash crops, governments sought to define a more positive solution to the problem of agricultural revenues for the state and for rural people. The solution was to induce producers to adopt improved methods of production. In effect this meant that directly or indirectly the government would exert influence not only over marketing of crops, but over the production process itself. The idea was not entirely new. Colonial governments already had tried a range of means to change production, from the relatively indirect and persuasion-oriented extension services established by Britain to the directly administered *paysannat* with detailed rules about crop rotations and farming practices in regions of the Belgian Congo. Without investment in agriculture and without any political participation by members, the *paysannat* became yet another form of coerced crop production (Jewsiewicki 1980).

The independent governments could use their control over marketing and their new moral authority to bring peasant farmers to adopt new methods. To succeed, a programme had to meet several stringent criteria. In the first place the government services had to have a technical package that worked. And it had to work in the particular agronomic and social environment in which it was being applied. Second, the government had to have the means to make the material elements of the package – the seed, fertilizer, and tools – available to the producers at the times they were required. Third, the producers had to have the means, usually including credit, necessary to acquire the material–technical package. Fourth, the government service had to be able to give the necessary informationto the peasant farmers attempting to use the new method. If any one of these conditions was lacking the programme could not succeed. In case after case one or another condition was not met. Very often the technical package was faulty or not applicable in the environment where it was applied. Or, the administrative and transportation infrastructure kept the seed or fertilizer from arriving at the right time. Or, the credit system failed and the inputs were restricted to very few producers. Or, the inputs were supplied but the information on how to use them was not there when the peasant farmer set to work in his or her fields (Lele 1975).

Failure drove governments to attempt rural development projects with increasingly direct control over production. Several methods, listed here in order of increasing central direction, have been employed.

1. *Laissez-faire* or benign neglect.
2. Information and advice from extension agents.
3. Strong supervision and instruction from extension agents.
4. Credit conditioned on adopting specific farming methods.
5. Market access conditioned on adopting specified methods.
6. Contracting with buyer to adopt farming methods.
7. Contract stipulating that buyer will carry out methods if peasant farmer does not.
8. Scheme under central control with entry conditioned on adopting new methods.

9. Scheme placing day-to-day operations of farmers under central administrative control.
10. Scheme under central control employing hired labour.

The list shows that a wide range of degrees of control is exemplified by different kinds of rural development projects in Africa. They all assume that the administrators of the project know better how to farm efficiently than do the farmers themselves. Governments claim they are seeking to increase productivity, but the matter is not so straightforward. Research on factory production has shown that even under private capital, a second motive shapes the way capital administers production: to control labour and to prevent political action which might compromise the dominant position of capital (Burawoy 1985).

There is every reason to believe African governments or their rural development agencies are similarly motivated. Governments have several reasons to want to control peasant-farming production: they may believe they can improve productivity, but even if that fails they can gain maximum control over the profits, use access to means of production to reward faithful followers, direct resources to production for the markets they choose, fit the activity into the most promising applications for external aid, and provide jobs for civil servants and contracts for business and political associates.

In recent years an alternative to government control over agricultural production is receiving growing attention. In international financial agencies, among African business groups, and even in government many now argue that the displacement of control over agriculture from peasant farmers and government agencies to capitalists is a precondition for decisive improvement in productivity. To them it is self-evident that for capital the profit motive looms larger and the political agenda is more confined to keeping labour quiet and malleable. Multinational capital has additional attractions: it can mobilize large investments, it has ready access to the latest technologies and forms of organization, and it maintains connections with major export markets. The corresponding fear is that a multinational company will use its control to profit the company at the expense of the host country. Perhaps local private capital is best situated to propel agricultural change in a productive direction. After all, peasant farmer entrepreneurs in the classic mould established cocoa production in Ghana, and elements of similar progressive economic innovation occurred in Kenya and elsewhere. Some observers believe that

In retrospect, colonial attempts to introduce capitalism were half-hearted when compared to what a number of African governments are doing. Unencumbered by the fear of the emergence of an indigenous bourgeoisie or 'native revolts' over land rights, African governments are changing land tenure systems at a pace that would have made many a colonialist cringe. (Mkandawire 1987, 21)

But consistent and reliable breakthroughs by an African capitalist farming class are precious few. As noted above, the opportunity for accumulation has been much greater in trade, transport, and administration than in farming. The historic bias in the marketing system against the peasant producers and in favour of settlers, colonial trading companies, and wage labour employers goes far to explain the limited development of African agrarian capital. Even if this bias were to be removed, there are further questions about whether control of agriculture by government or by private capital will lead to better production. The capitalists may have a mistaken idea about how to improve productivity. They may be mesmerized by the achievements of capitalist agriculture in North America and Europe and apply these methods to places where conditions are altogether different. There are many examples of the misapplication of temperate region methods to tropical environments. With the best of capitalist motives, governments and capitalists can still do the wrong thing. Moreover, peasant farming may resist change for its own internal social and cultural reasons. Examining some of the attempts to control peasant farming will lay the groundwork for a discussion of the politics of change in peasant farming in chapters 6, 7, and 8.

Improving smallholder farming

The first three types of effort to influence production listed above are all variants of smallholder improvement policies. Peasant producers retain an arm's length relationship with the marketing and supply agencies with which they deal. They remain independent entities making their own decisions, but they are given new possibilities and better information. An agricultural extension service sends agents to the homes and fields of the farmers to tell them what they can do to improve their production and their earnings within the limits of the land, labour, and tools they control and the markets and supply networks they have available.

As the list of methods of government intervention noted above makes clear, it is a short step from suggesting changes in farming method to enforcing them. One kind of pressure is simple urging and strong recommendation by the extension agent who has the trappings of government authority. The next steps are to offer credit or access to market on condition that the inputs be purchased and the practices be followed. An administrator of the French firm, SATEC, complained to me in 1964 that his company could not do a proper job of the extension work it was contracted to do in Senegal because it had no 'grip' on the producers. He would have preferred to control credit as well as extension services. Credit, he explained, was like a lever giving much more control over productive practices than simple persuasion could muster.

Marketing cooperatives have often tried to use control over credit as a source of influence over investment. We have seen that market producers very often participated in a regular cycle of debt and repayment. To feed and clothe themselves in the months before the new crop was sold, and sometimes to pay the cost (for seed and labour) of planting the new crop, peasant farmers would borrow from merchants. In the case of Senegal, the cooperatives were (from 1965–1983) given a monopoly on the purchase of groundnuts. They were also given the job of allocating credit, something private merchants were now reluctant to do since they no longer could buy the crop which was the only guarantee most producers could offer to secure their debt. The cooperatives, by policy, restricted their loans to agricultural tools and inputs. Extension agents encouraged peasant farmers to buy inputs on credit, knowing that the cooperatives would not be allowed to buy peanuts until the membership as a whole repaid 80 or 90 per cent of the outstanding debt (Schumacher 1975). Similar leverage was widely used by marketing institutions to encourage, if not to enforce, improved farming methods.

The advice of extension agents in Africa did not become famous for its high quality. The underlying assumption was that the peasant farmers did not know their job very well and would need some basic advice on early planting, the benefits of producing for the market, and the benefits of selected seed and other inputs. Often the advice was not well founded. To the extent that the advice was useful, it was almost inevitably biased in favour of the larger producers. They had more in common with the agents culturally and they had the means and the flexibility to invest in new methods. They could take advantage of the credit made available or they could save and invest or borrow and invest on their own. Moreover, the extension agents were too few to try to reach all peasant farmers, and they knew that the impact on production of influencing one large producer was greater than the impact of influencing a small producer (Lele 1975, 62–80).

Contract farming

In order to gain firmer control over the production practices of peasant farmers, particularly for crops like tobacco and tea which require especially close attention, marketing and manufacturing companies like British and American Tobacco and Brooke Bond tea company initiated a system in which producers would contract with the company not only to deliver the crops, but also to follow specified procedures for producing and handling them. In return the company agrees to buy the crop, often at a stated price, and it takes on the task of supervising the contract. In some cases it even will carry out tasks neglected by the producers, charging the cost of the work to the account of the producer in question (Halfani and Barker 1984, 48–51).

In contract farming the process of submitting production to control by capital is carried much farther than it is in agricultural extension: the operations of production are determined by the buying agency. Legally the producer is still independent and exercises the choice of whether to contract or not. In practice the choice may be severely restricted; other buyers and other cash crops may not be available, while the need to earn a cash income is imperious. The relationship of contract farmers to the agency with which they contract raises fascinating practical and theoretical questions. Under what conditions does it raise productivity and income for the farmers? When is it a way to increase political, social, and economic control? Under what conditions does it encourage peasant farmers to organize and assert their common interest against the contracting agency? What happens to social and community interests as the economic motives of the buyers shape more and more production decisions, decisions which also shape community life? As contract farming becomes more common in Africa, research on questions such as these becomes more imperative.

Centrally managed schemes

While, formally speaking, contract farming leaves the farmers as independent operators, centrally managed development projects can convert peasant farmers into scheme operatives. On smaller or more decentralized schemes some elements of independent farming or contract farming may be preserved. As a condition of their entry or membership, households may be required to farm certain land in certain ways. In legal terms they may be regarded as tenants whose tenancy is conditioned upon the performance of certain tasks. The ability of members or tenants to determine their own operations varies from scheme to scheme and over time on the same scheme, but very often production activity is highly controlled. Such in particular is the case with irrigation schemes where many farm operations are determined by the delivery of water. The rights of scheme members to participate in running the scheme and to make decisions for it is an important issue over which conflict between members and management is likely (Barnett 1977).

In some cases tenants have strong legal rights to their place in the scheme and they are able to hire labour for many of the farming operations. In the Gezira scheme in Sudan many tenants have become something like subcontracting junior managers. They have to follow scheme rules about crop acreages and times for planting and weeding. But they hire workers to do the operations specified by the scheme administrators. The tenant family lives in scheme housing and oversees production of both food and cash crops. To that extent it is still a peasant farming unit. But the basic farming decisions are made by the scheme and the basic work is done by employees of the tenant. The peasant farmer in this case becomes akin to a subcontracting agent, neither worker nor owner. Can we here speak of full control of production by capital? Again, the many types of schemes and their very diverse results are fitting subjects for further comparative research.

The accumulation of farming capital

On the whole the big accumulators of capital from the African export farming systems have been trading companies and governments. Accumulation gives the power to shape production. These accumulators have seldom channelled the capacity to shape production toward agriculture itself. Trading companies have expanded in other markets including the metropolitan one. Governments have favoured industry, infrastructure, and government services. Where they have invested in agriculture they have often preferred large, centrally administered schemes. Nevertheless, certain members of peasant-farming communities have succeeded in accumulating capital. They are the visible beneficiaries of social differentiation and moving forces in the restructuring of rural society.

In the case of higher-value tree crops like cocoa, coffee, and tea, the creation of farms signifies substantial accumulation of capital, derived mainly from the labour of clearing land, planting seedlings, and tending the seedlings until maturity. For annual crops the creation of the farm is usually a smaller investment, but the purchase of equipment such as ploughs and seeders, carts, or even hoes and machetes sets some producers apart from others. In many areas of rural Africa investment in cattle is a common way to store savings and to establish social ties. In times of drought or hardship the possession of a herd of cattle may spell the difference between surviving on the land or abandoning it for the hope of a city job. In more normal times the herd is a mark of wealth and stability, but it is not a kind of capital that is easy to mobilize for the improvement of agriculture. The fact remains that the road to greater wealth and power in the marketplace passes from farming to trade, transport, and what might be called political accumulation, much more often than it passes through investment in bigger and better farming.

The history of peasant farmer relations with colonial and independent states in Africa, as it has been sketched in chapter 4, and the account of market relationships given in this chapter demonstrate that the market is only part of the story of peasant-farmer politics. Patronage, violence, organization, leadership, ecology, gender relations, age relations, and practices of local political bodies also enter the equation. Nor can their rich range of activity be reduced to matters of peasant-farmer values. The next chapter goes beyond the market argument to seek a fuller understanding of the social economy of peasant-farmer politics.

§ 6 §

COMMUNITIES UNDER STRESS

The market dynamic is undoubtedly a powerful force driving and shaping the politics of peasant farming, but it is by no means the whole story. The last chapter noted the stratification of market power among peasant farmers who are more or less successful in producing for the market. It noted the structuring of wealth and influence alongside the marketing system as some peasant farmers add transport, commerce, and money-lending to their agricultural activities. Differences of wealth and social interest begin to shape political interests, power, and conflicts within the local community and between local communities and the state. The changes in the politics of peasant-farming families, their communities, and their relations with the wider society and the government reach deeper and further than a purely market-oriented analysis is able to reveal. Several models have been put forward which seek, by deliberate simplification, to capture the essential social forces at work in Africa's agrarian change. Examining some of these models will help to reveal the directions in which to seek a more complete perspective on the situation of peasant farmers and peasant-farming communities. They are, the chapter argues, communities under stress. Before turning to models of the forces which control peasant farming it will help to set out the broad pattern of change which the models aspire to explain.

FINDING THE FORCES OF CHANGE

The two great periods of foundation of peasant-farming regions in Africa were separated by two generations of depression and war. The first was the early 1900s while colonial administration was being wrestled into place in most of the colonies. Expansion and self-perpetuating growth or maintenance followed in the 1920s. The depression of the 1930s brought stagnation and crisis which continued until the end of World War Two. Some of the old cash-crop regions (cocoa and peanuts in West Africa) experienced a revival in the early post-war period and other new regions (coffee in Angola and Côte d'Ivoire) were initiated then, either as extensions and expansions of old ones, or as wholly new regions. Around 1960, the time of independence, growth measured for sub-Saharan Africa as a whole slowed or stopped, and in the 1970s many regions (especially those burdened by drought and war) had entered a state of crisis. In the 1980s a predicament of inadequate production grips peasant farming in most of sub-Saharan Africa, while in any given year an active crisis of starvation, emigration, and emergency relief operations afflicts several large regions and millions of peasant farmers.

Three different models summarize the major perspectives on the pressures acting upon peasant farming communities (Table 7). One perspective focuses on *market forces* and rational maximizing behaviour. Another stresses the influence of *peasant values*. A third centres on the *forces of articulation* linking capitalist and precapitalist social relations. Another explanation examines the way social, economic, and ecological forces can come to undermine the ability of peasant farming units to sustain themselves by subjecting them to a *simple reproduction squeeze*. This last explanation does not attempt to model

Table 7 *Models of peasant farming*

Market forces	Peasant values	Articulation
Motive of peasant farmers is to maximize income.	Motive of peasants is to protect family and its values.	Motive is to sustain relations and beliefs of domination and community.
Production unit organized like a small firm, deploying labour, land, tools for income	Work divided by gender and age according to community tradition.	Production dominated by usually male family heads and senior lineages. Managed to preserve domination.
Links to other peasant farmers are very localized and politically ineffective. Organizing is especially difficult for poorer producers.	Links to surrounding peasant farming communities via kinship networks and ethnic loyalty.	Links to other peasant farmers through lineage hierarchies, other systems of stratification and kinship ties.
Links to national society through markets for farm products and farm inputs as well as consumption goods, and through administrative services.	Links to wider political society through patronage networks and ethnic bargaining.	National links through class alliances of local dominant groups with national merchant capital.
Biased against peasant farmers as urban coalition sets low food prices	Biased toward insulation from market forces as peasant farmers	Class alliance protects local domination and pre-capitalist

Table 7 *(cont.)*

Market forces	Peasant values	Articulation
and places high taxes on agricultural exports.	maintain exit option and draw government into patronage politics	farming methods against full transformation of land and labour into commodities, favouring personalist style of local politics.
Best avenue of reform is to remove market biases against rural producers. A rural elite of large farmers connected with urban politics may help the reform prospects.	Progressive reform requires submitting peasant farmers to external control by a capitalist class operating in terms of market rationality.	Gradual reform can be expected as peasant farming is subsumed by more productive capitalist tendencies. Alternatively, a peasant-worker alliance might break through the protection of precapitalist domination.

peasant-farming society; it tries to depict the pattern of change which peasant farmers engaged with market forces experience.

Market forces and maximizing choices

Economists have long viewed peasant farmers, like other producers, as income maximizers. There has been controversy, however, over the ability of peasant farming to transform the production process and to increase productivity very rapidly. The 'vent-for-surplus' analysis of the development of export agriculture argued that new transportation routes and new market opportunities opened non-market producers to the market–commodity circuit. Land and labour uncommitted to productive use was mobilized by new demand on overseas markets and motivated by new purchasing opportunities. In this view cash-crop zone farming was added with few effects on the pre-existing circuits: no new labour supply was needed, no decrease in the production of traditional goods and services would follow, and no major change in the technology or organization of farming was required. The market simply mobilized land, labour, and other factors of production for expanded output. Vent-for-surplus tended to justify the colonial economy by arguing that the market opportunities brought by the colonial regime drew out productive capacities which the old system left dormant.

Research shows that in fact, peasant farmers who entered market production transformed their social relations in many important ways. In the first place, the supply of labour in export crop zones was very sharply increased through seasonal and permanent immigration. Recent research estimates, for example, that between 1920 and 1970 three million peasant farmers left the interior regions of West Africa to settle permanently in the groundnut regions of Senegal and Gambia and the cocoa and coffee regions of Ghana and Côte d'Ivoire (Amin 1974, 98–124). In addition there was significant population growth in the continent as a whole. In the second place, local investment was needed to plant new crops and to bring more land under cultivation. The planting of tree crops was a considerable investment in which a great deal of labour was capitalized and new techniques of production were learned. The new annual cash crops required some innovation in production techniques as well and investment in local transportation networks and storage depots (Levi and Havinden 1982, 41–45). In the third place, and most significantly, there was the change in labour relations brought about in the new peasant-farming zones. Wage labour, sharecropping, and labour rental became common. Production units organized according to kinship, age, and gender altered the allocation of tasks under the new requirements for labour. Finally, food-crop production was sometimes undermined by the adoption of cash cropping, particularly in the case of non-edible crops, and of annual cash crops in dry grain-farming zones (Tosh 1980; Levi and Havinden 1982, 127).

Current versions of the idea that peasant farmers act to maximize their incomes on the markets they face takes account of the transformation the peasant farmers have undergone and includes the view that they will continue to invest in production and to change their farming methods. They need, however, to be convinced that the changes will expand their income in a reliable way. The onus is placed on research and extension to show peasant farmers what the improved methods are and on prices to signal the benefits they will bring.

One particular version of the market forces perspective is of interest here: the public-choice perspective. It takes a broad political–economic view of rational maximizing choices and of the context in which they are made. In particular, it adds to the reasoning about economic behaviour a logic of political organization. Economically, it holds that peasant farmers respond not only by applying existing resources and techniques to the meeting of new demands; they also invest and improve production when the incentives are strong and certain enough to overcome the rational fear of failure. Politically, it postulates that individual peasant farmers, like merchants and government officials, invest their labour in political activity to protect their incomes. Peasant farmers in comparison to the groups with which they deal face high organizing costs because they are numerous and geographically dispersed, and because they must stay on their farms to work much of the time. Moreover, each individual in the large group has a small voice. Merchants and officials, in comparison, find political organizing cheaper. In addition they are often in a position to use monopoly power to alter prices in their favour. They can collect monopoly rents in the form of bribes, payoffs, favours, and distorted prices (Bates 1981).

The peasant farmers best able to defend themselves politically, on this analysis, are the larger, more mobile, and better connected farmers. In defending their own incomes, it follows, they will defend the incomes of many smaller farmers. Large and small alike will benefit from higher crop prices, lower marketing costs, cheaper input costs. Therefore, large farmers become the valid representatives of peasant-farmer interests and, the argument concludes, a viable way to increase the political weight of peasant farming is to encourage the emergence of a class of large farmers (Bates 1981).

While a distinct improvement over the older market models, the public choice model does not readily express four important kinds of change in peasant farming. One is the changing allocation of labour within production units and the tensions and conflicts it produces. A second is the change in community relations which separates the interests of large farmers from small and failing farmers. Where large farmers employ the weaker producers, where they assert new religious and social values, and where they knit strong ties with administrative and trading classes to the exclusion of the smaller farmers, the logic of community divisions needs to have a place in any analysis of peasant farmer activity. A third kind of change which the public choice model ignores is the quality of leadership which makes such a great difference when there are latent grievances and inchoate tensions which may or may not achieve political expression. Finally, there is a question about whether all peasant farmers are income maximizers, as the focus on market forces assumes. Are not values of security and family solidarity in some cases dominant?

In principle, public choice analysis can meet these criticisms. It can study the context of choice within peasant-farming units and within communities. It can add variables like quality of leadership, and goals like security to its behavioural models. However, analysis rarely makes these refinements for the good reason that they detract from the powerful simplicity of an analysis which sees a population of income-maximizing farming units each separately facing a limited set of markets.

Peasant values

Peasant values are given a central place in another view of change in peasant-farming communities. The view holds that peasant farmers have social commitments in which the maintenance of good family relations and community harmony are primary goals. Depending on the circumstances and the precise community values in question, peasant farmers are blocked from maximizing income by the web of peasant values. Part of the problem of improving peasant farming, in this view, is accomplishing a change in basic social commitments. Otherwise, economic progress is repeatedly thwarted by the mobilization of community values under threat. Short of changing values, peasant farming will only improve production dramatically if it is brought under the control of economically-progressive classes. The rift between peasant farmers and the modernizing elites, in this perspective, will be very difficult to bridge (Hyden 1980).

Some analysts of peasant values affirm that the content

of social commitments differs among peasant farmers of different cultural groups. Some, they argue, have values closer to those assumed in the market forces model. For example the instrumental values of the Baganda were said to adapt more easily to modern organization and production than the ends-oriented values of the Asante (Apter 1965, chapter 3). And the egalitarian values of the Kikuyu and the Igbo are said to adapt quite readily to populist forms of political organization. However, the fact that social values and social commitments change over time, partly as a result of experience with cash crop agriculture and other social innovations, casts doubt on the idea that values are simple social givens.

A much cited recent form of the peasant values model is the argument, referred to in the last chapter, that the peasantry in Africa is 'uncaptured', or autonomous from other classes (Hyden 1980). Here the distinctive values of the peasantry are tied to the distinctive self-provisioning economy of peasants. Self-provisioning gives peasant farmers a sense of economic autonomy and a strong belief in the survival and harmony of the family and the local community. They are skeptical of economic innovation and rapid improvement of productivity. Instead they resist necessary changes in the uses of land and property and in the way production is organized. Moreover, peasant values do not match the requirements of administrative rationality. They focus on personal loyalty and family solidarity rather than on overall fairness and efficient goal attainment. They stress community services rather than economic production. As a result, governments are led into bidding for peasant-farmer support with services, and their administrative operations are infected with debilitating claims for personal and family favours.

The emphasis on peasant values leads analysis of the peasant problem in the direction of prescribing ways in which the values of economic achievement can be taught or, if that is not possible, then imposed, perhaps through an authoritarian government or an emergent class of agrarian capitalists. The argument is severely undermined by the fact that on many cash crop markets peasant farmers are price-responsive and appear to act very much like maximizers (Levi and Havinden 1982, 43–45 and 112–114). In what sense are they, then, 'uncaptured'? Moreover, in conditions of collapsing market institutions, peasant farmers often go to great lengths to establish some kind of marketing system, whether legal or illegal, formal or informal. If they have great economic autonomy – the exit option – many peasant farmers seem most reluctant to run for the exit even when the market economy is in shambles.

The rules of strict administrative rationality may be widely rejected in Africa, but no more among peasant farmers than among urban dwellers. The idea that African peasant farmers have economic and social values significantly different from those of wage workers or the urban self-employed is pure supposition.

The forces of articulation

Like the notion of peasant values, the idea of 'articulation of modes of production' holds that in rural Africa a politically and economically dominant capitalist society incorporates a subordinate precapitalist society. However, articulation places not a complex of values but a set of forces and relations of production at the centre of its conception of capitalism and pre-capitalism. The idea of articulation draws attention to the question of precisely how the two distinct modes of production are linked. What binds them together, and with what effects upon each mode of production? How does the pattern of binding evolve over time (Foster-Carter 1978)?

Studies employing the idea of articulation have revealed much about the ways in which labour is recruited, tasks are assigned, and products are allocated. Rural producers, according to one influential account, were first subjected to the forced appropriation of labour and products. Then, class alliances were struck between representatives of capital and the dominant classes or dominant social forces of the precapitalist mode of production, in the person of chiefs, heads of clans, and powerful lineages. In a third phase, a direct relation was established between merchant capital (in the form of trading companies and their agents) and lineage-based production units. The production units held land and organized labour according to precapitalist principles, but they also exchanged a portion of their production on a capitalist market (Rey 1973).

The articulation model in sophisticated hands is a most interesting approach to many issues of peasant producers in Africa (Wolpe 1980). Yet, it suffers from a methodological difficulty. Part of the utility of the idea of mode of production is that it is more than a type of production unit; it identifies the dynamic principle of a whole society over a long period of historical change. Marx, for example, gave a convincing account of the dynamic principles of the capitalist mode of production. The idea of different modes of production is not designed to sort out with much accuracy the capitalist from the non-capitalist elements in a complex and changing local reality. At what point does bridewealth cease to be a symbol of reciprocal obligations between two joined groups of kin and become the price for obtaining control over a unit of labour? When does the chief's power of trusteeship over common land turn into ownership of the means of production? These questions cannot be given any precise answers, although the search for answers will turn up fascinating information about the strains and conflicts brought about by rural change.

The idea of the articulation of mode of production has another logical problem. It holds that the capitalist mode of production is dominant in the sense that it imparts the major dynamic of economic change through its regulation of the accumulation or investment, which shapes change in production. What then of the precapitalist modes of production which have lost that dynamic capacity? Have they not therefore ceased to be modes of production, properly speaking? The model faces a final issue of method: in its large sense a mode of production is supposed to embody a set of laws of motion for a society. Where are to be discovered the laws of motion for a mixed or articulated social formation? For the purposes of understanding the way agricultural society in Africa is changing, the search for the laws of motion of a social formation which combines capitalist and non-capitalist relations of production is not a promising avenue of inquiry. For mixed social formations abstract analysis will inevitably discover ambiguous laws of motion. From the scholarly debate we can, nevertheless, extract a useful starting point for empirical study: an acknowledgment that capitalist market forces do interact with social relationships whose inspiration and sustenance have non-market and non-capitalist sources. This approach seeks to understand the pattern of pressures which market forces and community practices generate for peasant farmers.

The simple reproduction squeeze

Chapter 3 argued that peasant farmers operate on two, and often three economic circuits. On the domestic circuit they supply themselves with food, shelter, and household goods, using their own tools and labour. On the market circuit they buy inputs and consumption goods and grow crops for sale. On the wage labour circuit some of them sell labour for wages or other income. The three circuits are not easily separated. For example, purchased inputs and tools may be used for production of food for family consumption and the labour sold for wages is lost to cash crop production. Operating on three circuits gives producers some flexibility in their relation to market production. If prices for marketable produce are high and stable, peasant farmers are likely to commit more of their land and labour to that circuit, perhaps at the expense of the others. On the other hand, if prices for the cash crop are low and unreliable, producers may well reduce their commitment to that circuit and raise their participation in the others.

Although it may be flexible and rational, peasant farming is still subject to pressures and stresses. A frequent pattern has been labelled the 'simple reproduction squeeze' (Bernstein 1979). It can be related to four stages of incorporation into market production: after the possibly forced induction into market production (stage 1), maintaining the circuit of cash crop production (stage 2) seems beneficial. The time taken from social activity and from domestic production is repaid by cash income, which is wonderfully versatile in what it will buy. Cash-crop production may continue to expand, motivated by the positive gains of a cash income and reinforced by imposed cash needs such as tax payment. For some zones and for some producers, however, harder times (stage 3) often follow. The price to producers of the cash crop begins to fall as a consequence of the cycle of world production and demand, or as a result of taxation or monopoly price discrimination against producers. Also, productivity falls as land shows the effects of shorter fallow periods or as a cycle of poor rainfall appears. Peasant farms face the question of how to respond to a shrinking income per unit of labour. All the options are stressful and the stresses are more profound and complex than is commonly recognized. Much more than the return to labour is at stake. Where such stresses affect not just the poor farmers and not just certain localities, but become widespread, there is a generalized crisis (stage 4) which calls a whole regional political economy into question.

Entering cash crop production already brings the division of tasks within the production unit under pressure. Very often men take charge of cash-crop production, passing a larger burden to women. They may reduce their labour on food crops. Certainly those who go away to earn wages withdraw labour from the domestic circuit and damage its productivity. In managing the cash-crop fields the (usually male) head of the household will ask for labour on the part of the women and young men of the production group. This new demand for labour and the issue of control of the resulting earnings are often sources of tension in the producing group. Much research shows that women peasant farmers frequently bear the brunt of pressures from the changes brought about by cash crop production and the sending away of labour for wage employment. There is a rise in the proportion of female household heads who very often farm with insufficient help from male kin. Women are pressed to continue their usual household work of cooking, caring for children, and cleaning while they also take even greater responsibility for food-crop production. In addition women are asked to do work on cash crops without getting commensurate control over the earnings (Bryson 1981).

A drop in earnings for the same labour and land commitment only increases the tensions. One response is to work even harder at both food production and cash-crop production in order to retain the same income. Another response is to shift to more domestic production. On the whole, the result is to try to get more productivity out of the same land and labour. Intensifying production in many cases adds to ecological degradation. Population growth, cash-crop acreage, monocrop tillage practices, and the loss of agricultural land to other uses push peasant farmers to more intense forms of cultivation and, often enough, to significant environmental damage. The result is to place stress on the social relations that regulate the acquisition of land and the allocation of labour. But the stress is not only material, not only agronomic and economic; it is moral as well. At issue in the eyes of some community members is a way of life: customs and practices about the work done by men and women, young people and adults, and about the way decisions are made and power is exercised.

In many agricultural regions of Africa, the male head of a household has strong hierarchical authority over the women and younger men who compose the junior membership of the production unit. On many matters the head of the family can give orders and expect them to be obeyed; he usually directs work on a set of fields devoted to crops which are used to support the unit as a whole. Cash crops are different from crops grown for own use in one crucial respect: there is no upper limit of useful production. Moreover the value produced in cash-crop farming is pre-eminently consumable by individuals. Cash-crop production introduces a new and more intense clash between the autonomy of junior members and the authority and power of the head of the unit (or in some cases, its collective power and authority). Junior members want to control the earnings their work creates; the head wants to translate his control over family labour into earnings for which there is no particular reasonable upper limit.

The cumulative and recurrent pattern of pressures on peasant-farming units goes beyond the simple reproduction squeeze to a more general political–economic stress on production units and peasant-farming communities. Poor producer prices, high population growth, and a dearth of relevant technical research have made the squeeze a widespread experience among Africa's peasant farmers. Very often the micropolitical pressures associated with the squeeze are contained within the production unit, or else their consequences are only indirectly political. Young people may leave their fathers' production groups at a young age. Wives may seek divorce more frequently. Elders may try to raise bridewealth to a very high value in order to discourage the attempts of young people to assert their autonomy at a young age. The eventual political manifestation may be the organization of new political groups, for example a youth association with the reduction or elimination of bridewealth as one of its objectives, or a women's group dedicated to strengthening the social and political voice of women.

Other social and political consequences of such pressures may be less direct. The current crisis on family farms in the grain belt of North America has provoked drinking, wife battering, and suicide. The social consequences of similar pressures among peasant farmers in Africa should be the object of research and informed thinking about policy changes (Tabatabai 1986). Conflict and uncertainty over authority and division of tasks in the household, along with the pressures of economic hardship in sub-Saharan Africa may well contribute to alcohol abuse and to the violence of husbands against their wives. But these are not the only sources of stress by any means.

POLITICAL PRESSURES

Only some of the pressures on peasant-farming communities are the outgrowth of the stresses on production units noted above. Others have their origin in the political history of the peasant-farming zones. In the past generation in many of these communities the precolonial authorities were defeated and the system of rule was dismantled or allowed to function in a modified or severely constricted way in conjunction with colonial administration. Older standards and lines of authority retain some force and often blend with newer forms of leadership. Part of the activity of nationalist politics in many peasant-farming zones was the creation of new political networks and processes which took into account old systems of authority, either by incorporating them or by trying to marginalize them.

The need for new networks and new or combined rules and customs was augmented by the immigration and relocation of people typical of the evolution of peasant-farming zones. Sometimes the zone was founded by immigrants in an area where the new and dynamic cash-crop producers achieved precedence over a sparse local population less interested in the new economic possibilities. Such was the case with parts of the cocoa zone of Ghana (Hill 1963).

In other places immigrants came as agricultural workers, labour tenants, or settlers. Those who stayed resided in special villages, special neighbourhoods, or in scattered residences. Very often some sort of corporate identity was retained at least for a time. Ethnic mixing also means the cohabitation of different idioms and customs of politics. Not only are languages different, but so are ideas about kinds of authority, bases of leadership, ways to carry on political discussions, and principles of equality and inequality.

Another source of differences within peasant-farming communities is the different ways production units intersect with the wage-market economy. Some are market oriented. They see the opportunity for expanded income given by market production. For them it is sensible to invest in new tools, selected seeds, fertilizers, and pesticides. In a number of times and places the market-oriented group has taken the lead and impressed its preferences on a whole region. Elsewhere they are a distinct minority: the progressive farmers dear to the hearts of advocates of capitalist development.

Other production units are self-provisioning oriented. They keep their cash-crop commitment to a minimum and rely on a large harvest of sorghum, maize, rice, plantains, yams, or manioc to supply basic nourishment. They may also grow many of the vegetables and condiments, and even the meat, they like to have. Some whole regions or communities by preference or by force of circumstance have chosen not to stress cash crops. In regions with mixed tendencies those who resist cash crops may move to the fringes of the zone where large grain fields can still be planted, where bush fallowing can still be practised, and where the opportunity for hunting and collecting wild food is greater (Knight 1974). In most cash-crop zones there have been periods when the conflict between advocates and resistors of the new way was strong. To those for whom the pursuit of cash seemed wrong and immoral the cash-crop farmers, especially those with expanding incomes, new consumer goods, and a changing way of life might seem a threat. Coffee fields might be sabotaged or witchcraft employed to bring the offending production unit into line. Later, when the fear of novelty has worn away, tensions reflecting a sense of social inequality may arise.

Similar suspicion might be shown toward peasant farmers who engage in wage labour in mines or plantations on a regular basis and those who have adopted trade or transport as a secondary occupation. Selling labour or engaging in truck and barter were often seen by peasant farmers as undignified pursuits. As a result of such resistance it was frequently the case within the newly multiethnic rural communities, that some ethnic groups would tend more strongly toward cash cropping, others toward trade, others toward wage labour migration, and others toward emphasis on self-provisioning.

Often cash-crop farming has gone along with religious change, frequently toward Islam or Christianity, and the new religion has usually entered the community in more than one variety. Both Islam and Christianity are highly political religions in the sense that their beliefs include ideas about authority, equality, justice, and membership in a community. They also create their own hierarchies of dignity and authority and their own kinds of leadership. Even when directed primarily toward religious ends, the activities of religious organizations impinge upon the exercise of secular power, especially so in societies where political power historically has been sacred as well as secular.

To sum up, peasant-farming communities face a daunting set of economic, cultural, social, and political tensions. The deep and rapid changes in rural Africa challenge basic beliefs about differences between men and women, old and young, kin and non-kin. They bring into question ideas about authority and obedience, and about the way public issues are defined and discussed. Above all they often bring fundamentally different views on these basic questions into dialogue and confrontation with one another. Such questions of value, belief, and practice are not divorced from material interests affected by changes in control of land and labour, from the opening and closing of avenues of occupational mobility, from the acquisition of new skills and technologies, or from changing markets for the products of peasant farming. Production activities, as chapter

3 already noted, are always carried out in terms of beliefs and ideas. In a particular community the ideas may be assumed and accepted for a long time, but a moment comes when some members of the community criticize, dispute, and reject formerly cherished conceptions. The next chapter examines some of the wider political issues faced by peasant-farming families, groups, and communities, and it considers the broad politics of the relation between peasant-farming communities and the wider political society, including the government.

PEASANT FARMERS AND THE 'BEGINNING OF POLITICS'

A peasant farmer in Senegal responding to my question about the activity of political parties in his region during the period after World War Two used the fitting phrase the 'beginning of politics'. He was right; the politics of decolonization in sub-Saharan Africa did begin the modern era of African politics. Decolonization gave different countries very distinct modern political traditions. These differ in fundamental experiences: much or little popular organization; strong regional and ethnic divisions or strong national party unity; a politics of cozy elite succession, energetic electoral combat, or arduous guerrilla warfare; political ideologies advocating continuity with colonial policies, socialist reform, or revolutionary rebirth. The diverse beginnings which shape politics and the place of peasant farmers in the political process also have a prehistory in the subterranean politics of colonial rule and in the precolonial ideas and practices which continue to inform the politics of the successor states.

PRECOLONIAL POLITICAL TRADITIONS

Africa is famous for the great variety of its precolonial political systems, ranging from democratic and egalitarian bands of hunter–gatherers, through networks of egalitarian communities of self-provisioning cultivators, to bureaucratic kingdoms with specialized trade and maufactures (Mair 1962; Fortes and Evans-Pritchard 1940). The very variety suggests one problem for political leaders in the post-colonial period: What kinds of political relationships should be emphasized and validated? An account of the more important kinds of precolonial political relationships which seem to find an echo in political life of modern peasant farmers is presented here. No attempt is made to show how a set of them may have been integrated in a single political system. They will be regarded, instead, as political resources from which political structures can be constructed, or a collection of resonant frequencies which political leaders can attempt to activate. The relative predominance of one kind of tradition or another differ from country to country and from region to region within a country. Such differences probably account for some of the divergence in the styles of politics which are apparent in Africa today.

In many precolonial African societies the vocabulary of politics was closely related to the language of kinship. Just as one's relations with other individuals followed from whether they were classified as brothers, sisters, cousins, or uncles; so clans and language groups were often treated as brother, cousin, or uncle peoples. Rulers or ruling clans were often categorized as older siblings or parents. Kinship, of course, remains a fundamental organizing principle in peasant farming communities. Is it surprising that in Tanzania the word for fellow citizen is *ndugu*, or brother? Or that Nyerere, the first president, is seen as the 'father' of the whole country?

Clientship, tributary status, and captivity or slavery were other kinds of political relationships from the precolonial period. The personal dependants of rulers were often an important base of their power. Armies were often formed from the slaves or captives of the ruler, and sometimes military leaders of slave status became very powerful. Slaves and other dependants also often worked the fields of the ruler and supplied an important economic support for rulership. Officials appointed to administer regions and districts in the kingdom were frequently personal dependants of the ruler. Even when they had an autonomous base as chief or elder among their own people, they might pay symbolic tribute as a mark of their recognition of the superiority of the central ruler. The patron owed certain obligations to the client (such as economic security for the client's family, for example), but the relationship was founded on the inferiority and relative weakness of the client. Although slavery and servile status have been abolished, distinctions among persons of royal, commoner, and inferior descent continue to influence attitudes and behaviour in much of Africa. Many social scientists see relationships of personal rule, patrimonial power, and patron-clientship as fundamental and even predominant elements in African politics (Jackson and Rosberg 1982; Sandbrook 1985).

Religion supplied further language and models of political relationships. In older African religions the chief was often a symbolic representative of the whole community in relation to its ancestors and descendants, and a bearer of supernatural powers. In community meetings, members rarely criticized the chief directly, nor did they bargain openly about frankly-stated competing interests. Political discussion was often indirect, stressing at least a façade of consensus and stated in a language influenced by the religious and ritual dimensions of political institutions (Geschiere 1982).

The religious side of politics became even more varied where Islam and Christianity entered the scene. In Islam there is a well-established language of law and government emphasizing the religious basis of political authority, and there are examples and justifications of military leadership. In both Islam and Christianity the idea of prophetic authority is strong. The appearance of religious prophets like the Mahdi in Sudan and Amadu Bamba in Senegal, both founders of powerful Muslim confraternities, and Simon Kimbangu in the Belgian Congo, founder of an influential syncretistic religion, has kept prophetic power alive in Africa. In Islam and, perhaps to a lesser degree, in Christianity there is also a vivid idea of the relationship between a teacher or master and his or her disciples. In Islam the authority of the master is absolute and the subjection of the disciple is total within the context of a teaching and learning environment, although teacher and disciple stand as equals in comparison to the greatness of Allah. Religious groups, ideas, and models still play a very lively part in African politics (Copans 1980; Demunter 1975).

Another kind of political relationship found in many African societies in the past was the age–grade association of men or women, or both. Persons in the same age group participated together in a ceremony of coming of age and formed a strong and egalitarian bond with one another. They could expect a loyalty from one another which they could not expect from outsiders. A similar loyalty is frequently observed today among members of the same school generation. Secret societies were another kind of group which stimulated and demanded special loyalty. They were a normal part of political life in many parts of Africa. Their membership, usually made up of older men, was co-opted; in concealed meetings they might make decisions about succession to leadership and other community matters. The colonial period spawned its own secret societies, such as the Freemasons, and the tradition certainly carries on today.

Ideas about the boundaries of political community often followed from the interpersonal definition of political relationships and political authority. To be recognized as a member of a certain kin group or a descendant of a certain ancestor was to have membership in the community. Alternatively, to be accepted as the dependant or client of a ruler could also be the basis of membership. The larger kingdoms and empires usually had a core area of strong direct authority and a wider region of suzerainty in which communities had a regular or episodic tributary status. The correlation of language or cultural ethnicity and political community was not strong at all. There were many multi-ethnic states and many ethnic groups were formed into a plurality of communities.

Fluidity and adaptability of political relationships is a part of the political traditions in many parts of Africa. Village communities grew, divided, and moved. Larger states prospered and expanded, and then, perhaps after suffering drought or defeat, grew poor and contracted. Families and communities often moved to a new area for reasons of warfare, climate, or political choice. Certainly the traditions of most communities contain stories of migrations, flights, heroic leaders emerging, the founding of new villages and states, and perhaps conquering and being conquered.

Even a brief review of precolonial political relationships reveals four striking differences from the liberal model of politics which is the implicit standard in political science textbooks. The first difference is the stress which was placed on personal relationships: kinship, clientship, and community membership. Studies of western politics recognize interpersonal networks, but do not integrate them with any care into the major political models (with the significant exception of the idea of a political machine). In African politics today the question of how to incorporate the obviously important interpersonal dimension remains controversial. In chapter 8 the issue will be discussed further.

A second characteristic of precolonial political practices in Africa was the range and variety of communities which were organized as political units. As a consequence there are many political pasts and many communities of loyalty to which appeal can still be made. A fundamental social pluralism is one of precolonial Africa's legacies to modern African politics.

A third characteristic of precolonial African politics – in part a corollary of the range of communities – was the variety of kinds of leadership it encompassed: family and community patriarchs; skilled warriors and inspired military commanders; carriers of ancestral wisdom and symbolism; persuasive speakers; founders of states and communities; religious teachers, saints, and prophets.

A fourth characteristic was relative cultural egalitarianism. The degree of equality varied. In some of the Muslim cultures there was specialized education for an elite in close contact with the wider traditions of Islam, and in some states founded by conquest the conquering group perpetuated its ethnic exclusivity. Yet even in such cases, language, music, dance, and stories were widely shared throughout the society. Very often the shared culture fostered a sense of social equality.

It is not surprising that echoes of the precolonial traditions are detectable in present-day African politics, especially in the rural sector. The recency of effective colonial rule in Africa and the continuing vitality of African society make continuity inevitable.

COLONIAL POLITICAL EXPERIENCE

Of course the precolonial patterns are only part of the repertoire of political traditions on which African societies draw. Colonial rule gave all of Africa direct experience of despotic authoritarianism and the marked privileges of an expatriate ruling caste. The despotic colonial adminis- tration had to work out a *modus vivendi* with the local societies in which peasant farming flourished. Whether the new authority was imposed by conquest (for example, in the groundnut region of Senegal and much of the cocoa region of Ghana) or by treaty (as was the case in the coffee and cotton zones of Uganda) the precolonial aristocracy, where one existed, usually retained a certain pre-eminence. In some cases it was incorporated into colonial local government institutions. Where hierarchical authority had not existed, it was introduced either through invented 'chiefs' or through district commissioners responsible to the colonial governor. Egalitarian societies often resisted the unwanted imposition of hierarchy.

Colonial rule also introduced developmental govern- ment to Africa. Earlier chapters showed that colonialism gave a powerful impulsion to the spread of peasant farming in Africa. Where market institutions were already active colonial governments strengthened and generalized them. Colonial rulers also gave crucial economic power to colonial trading companies, often taking that power from established African traders. Where market institutions were weaker, colonial governments set up market towns, encouraged the entry of trading companies, and intro- duced taxes to stimulate a need for cash income. However, especially in its waning decades, colonial rule went well beyond the promotion of markets: it created the first extensive examples in Africa of government actions designed to transform production. Even peasant farming was in some cases the target of reformist and developmen- tal policies. Examples of developmental projects include marketing and credit cooperatives, registration of land ownership, irrigated farming schemes, large-scale export

crop schemes, crop research, agricultural extension services, and administrative regulation of crops and farming
practices. The list is similar to the more ambitious list of
post-colonial development projects. Often the colonial
projects were the precursors of the post-colonial efforts.

Rapid economic change in colonial sub-Saharan Africa
proceeded under conditions of political despotism,
although in some cases the despotism was mediated by
institutions and aristocracies with local roots which had
formal or informal influence with the colonial administration. Colonial despotism did not stop peasant farmers
from responding to the dislocations of the profound
economic and social changes they were experiencing. In
some cases they organized protests against colonial actions. There were mass refusals by peasant farmers to sell
their export crops. The most famous was the cocoa holdup
in Ghana, but similar actions took place in Senegal,
Nigeria, and elsewhere. There were rural rebellions linked
to agricultural policies, from the Maji Maji rebellion in
Tanganyika, set off by compulsory cotton cultivation
in Tanzania in 1905, to the Land Freedom Army in Kenya in
the 1950s, demanding the restoration of African land
rights in the Kenya highlands. There were political actions
like the protests of African planters in Côte d'Ivoire
against the crop price and labour hiring privileges of
French estates. Some of the religious movements mentioned in the last chapter, such as the spread of Mouride
Islam in Senegal and Ansar Islam in Sudan were closely
related to the advance of cash-crop farming by Africans.

The tensions built into the colonial system of authoritarian alien rule took on a particular focus in the case of
peasant farmers who were subject to the power of the
colonial government on matters of vital economic and
cultural interest. Colonial government rules in Kenya
restricted access to land and enforced restrictions on crops

which peasant farmers could grow. Colonial policy in Côte d'Ivoire and Northern Rhodesia gave more favourable prices to European growers; Senegal allowed trading firms to set monopoly prices; and Mozambique and Obangui-Chari (now Central African Republic) enforced compulsory cultivation of cotton. In Tanzania the colonial government enforced cultivation practices like tie ridging and terracing in an often misconceived effort to stop erosion (Pratt 1976). The record of repugnant practices meant that there was usually a backlog of grievances for aspiring nationalist leaders to build upon in their efforts to unite urban and rural populations to fight against colonial rule.

To the earlier political traditions colonialism added four new elements. One was a model of bureaucratic despotism. The second was an example of developmental government. The third was an experience of rule by a class set apart by culture and by wealth. The fourth was the political framework of the nation-state. Nationalists went beyond the colonial model to make use of the ideas of representative government, democracy, and socialism in their fight for independence and in their construction of a system of government.

The political framework of the fight for independence imposed a difficult task upon the aspiring leadership. The nationalist intelligentsia was drawn from those educated in colonial, European, or American schools and they fought for independence under the banner of national self-determination and democracy. At the same time there was a tide of popular opposition to the despotic and exploitative acts of colonial government. The nationalists faced the task of organizing a political movement across the cultural gap which now separated government from ordinary people, of using or overcoming the older political traditions which still had salience, and of dealing with the pluralism of communities and loyalties. Nowhere were the difficulties greater than in initiating a politics of peasant farmers.

There were two main routes for the joining of national political leadership with peasant farmer rank and file. One was the electoral route in which the aim of organization was to win elections. The other was the guerrilla route in which the aim was to win a war against an intransigent colonial despotism.

ELECTORAL DECOLONIZATION

The 'beginning of politics' referred to by the Senegalese peasant farmer was the introduction of electoral politics to the countryside in 1946 with a franchise expanding to full adult suffrage in 1957 (Morgenthau 1964; 28). In most French and British colonies there was a period of 5, 10, or 15 years in which political parties formed and contested referenda and elections. In the Belgian Congo the electoral period was truncated to a few months. The elections of the decolonization period were the first occasion for drawing peasant farmers and other rural people into any kind of national political dialogue in the new countries. In a number of African colonies a peasant-farming component was a large and active segment of the nationalist political coalition. In the case of Senegal, Leopold Senghor left the Socialist Party of Senegal to found a new party, the Senegalese Democratic Bloc (BDS), with a new and strong rural base. He was particularly successful in gaining the support of what might be called the rural aristocracy of Muslim leaders and leading members of influential families (Morgenthau 1964, 152).

In Tanzania the Tanganyika African National Union (TANU) was helped in key peasant-farming areas by the active support of the leaders of marketing cooperatives and by several key members of old chiefly families who broke with the initial tendency of chiefs to support the colonial administration. In Sukumaland the resentment of peasant farmers against being cheated by traders and harassed by the administration fed into support for the fledgling cotton growers' associations which began to act as marketing and consumer cooperatives. The marketing cooperatives, already strong before TANU was formed in 1954, were the first mass organization in Sukumaland. Building on the older Tanganyika African Association, and, especially, the cooperative movement, TANU in 1955 became the leading organization of rural protest and representation. When it was banned in Lake Province, the Victoria Federation of Cooperative Unions, with its strong base among African traders and cotton growers, remained the main vehicle for political activism. The centrepiece of a wider conflict in the region was a bitter confrontation in Geita District in 1958 between citizens who were opposed to the local government and incensed by the introduction of a multiracial provincial council (with heavily disproportionate European representation) and the many agricultural regulations. A popular campaign of civil disobedience directed against the colonial government and the chiefs associated with it was championed by the national leadership of TANU. The local and the national victory of TANU owed much to the party's sensitivity to the grievances of peasant farmers (Maguire 1969, 196–234; Pratt 1976, 23–29).

In Ghana, Kwame Nkrumah broke away from the established urban leadership of the United Gold Coast Convention in much the same way that Senghor did in Senegal. Nkrumah's Convention People's Party (CPP), however, unlike Senghor's BDS, had the radical and populist 'youngmen' of the cities and towns as the major organizers and popularizers of the new political formation. After sweeping victories in elections in 1951 and 1954 (in which the small cocoa farmers were strong supporters), the CPP faced a new kind of opposition in the 1956 elections, which were forced by the British as a precondition for independence. The strength of the new National Liberation Movement (NLM) in the prime cocoa-growing region of Ashanti was a response to the CPP government's announced fixing of the cocoa price at 72 shillings per load for four years. The opposition party drew around it cocoa farmers, Ashanti chiefs, and conservative intelligentsia. Although the CPP won 71 of 104 seats, it came to independence without the firm backing of the economically crucial peasant farmers of the cocoa region. The cocoa farmers have remained a major political and economic problem in Ghana (Genoud 1969; Beckman 1976). In contrast, the Parti Démocratique de la Côte d'Ivoire (PDCI) was led by the head of the association of African cocoa farmers, Félix Houphouët-Boigny. The government formed by the PDCI retained the support of the cocoa and coffee farmers in the transition to independence. The larger-scale African farmers who hired labour and employed share-croppers were a major influence on the government in the first decade or more of independence (Morgenthau 1964, 166–218; Campbell 1978).

For those African countries in which elections were a major occasion for mass political action, the roles taken by peasant farmers were quite diverse. If in Côte d'Ivoire they had a leading place in the nationalist coalition, in Senegal and Tanzania they had an important supporting place in the governing coalition, and in Ghana they were first supporters and then a source of opposition to the governing coalition. In Nigeria, where different regional peasant-farming zones supported different parties, peasant farmers reinforced the regionalism which the colonial constitution forced onto the country (Watts and Shenton 1984).

In all the countries just named, the dialogue between aspiring leaders and peasant farmers focussed on symbolic issues of leadership and nationalism. However, it already touched on the specific grievances of peasant farmers against colonial controls over peasant farming and against unfair pricing and marketing practices. In many places a rural elite found itself a role as intermediary between the new nationalist leadership and the peasant farmers. Whether or not the peasant farmers were an integral part of the independence government coalition made a difference for the political patterns that evolved in the next two decades, but it was not always decisive. As Frantz Fanon had feared, nationalist leaders could gain rural electoral support and, once in power, turn away from peasant-farming needs. Fanon believed that the process of anti-colonial warfare could force a deeper unification of nationalist leadership with the peasant farming popular base (Fanon 1963, 101–102).

ARMED DECOLONIZATION

In Angola, Mozambique, Guinea-Bissau, and Zimbabwe, where colonial powers were less responsive to nationalist political pressures, nationalist leaders took up arms to fight for independence. They sought military and economic support from peasant farmers. The grievance of those whose land was taken and those who needed land to carry on their farming was a powerful stimulus to revolutionary action. In these countries only a change in government would change the laws of the land and lighten the oppressive weight of the settler population. In all four countries the settlers were pressing to entrench their position of economic and political privilege.

There was a strong nationalist leadership with a clear goal of political independence leading the guerrilla movements. The circumstance of colonial intransigence ruled out reformism. The nationalists who chose the path of guerrilla war were perforce revolutionaries. Having seen the way their nationalist predecessors in neighbouring countries had failed to make rapid economic and social progress and had developed governments notable for their instability, ineffectiveness, and corruption, the revolutionary leaders tried to put the often painful experience of the people who fought the guerrilla war and who supported the guerrilla armies to good political use.

In elections leaders need voters, but in anti-colonial warfare leaders need reliable troops, and troops need a reliable base of economic and social support. Especially in protracted war in the countryside, the pressure is on the leadership to knit a strong and supportive relationship with the rural population who must feed, house, and hide the fighters. Amilcar Cabral, leader of the African Party for the Independence of Guinea and Cape Verde (PAIGC), wrote and spoke trenchantly of the necessity of thorough and responsive political organization among the peasantry with methods and objectives adapted to the particular kind of rural society. Stratified societies with chiefs drawing power and prestige from their colonial administrative roles were less spontaneously anti-colonial than were egalitarian societies from whom forced labour had routinely been recruited. Regions which depended on the sale of cash crops had a real need to have their cash crop marketing protected, while regions with less commercial agriculture were less vulnerable to economic dislocation. For Cabral, the peasants, by their numbers and their sense of exploitation, were the physical base for the revolution; but the organizing and goal-setting revolutionary class was urban, made up of the workers and the revolutionary petty bourgeoisie (Cabral 1979, 133). Samora Machel, leading the Front for the Liberation of Mozambique (FRELIMO) in Mozambique, repeatedly stressed the importance of leaders listening to and respecting the ideas and needs of the people. Although the policy line came from the party, local leaders who could not show the people that the party policy merited support had failed to lead well. They, not the people, were presumed to be at fault (Machel 1976).

In the fighting itself there was real unity of peasants and leaders. However, regional differences were still a major concern and problem in all the cases in question. PAIGC had trouble holding the support of the Fulani aristocrats whose traditional standing had been confirmed and augmented by the Portuguese. FRELIMO had similar problems with supporters of Makonde chiefs. Part of the difficulty in both cases had to do with the interest of both elites in maintaining and expanding trade in agricultural exports. Both movements made a strong and partially successful effort to establish alternative export routes for cash crops. Despite such problem areas in Mozambique and Guinea-Bissau, basic political unity was achieved by dint of sensitive and deliberate leadership (Isaacman and Isaacman 1983, 95–96; Davidson 1969, 124).

In Zimbabwe and Angola the guerrilla movements did not achieve unity. Leadership, fighting forces, and mass base remained divided in both countries even at the moment of gaining power. However, in Zimbabwe the armies of the two main rival parties fought the war in separate parts of the country and had their external support zones in different bordering countries: the Zimbabwe African National Union (ZANU) operated from Mozambique and the Zimbabwe African People's Union (ZAPU) from Zambia. The negotiated settlement of the war was the occasion for a political truce (Astrow 1983).

In Angola the spark for the revolutionary uprising in all the Portuguese colonies was struck in a region where European settlers had begun to establish coffee estates in the 1950s. Those who rose against the settlers were workers on the coffee farms who felt doubly exploited: as peasants their land was stolen and as workers they were poorly paid and badly treated. The combination of immediate exploitation and being robbed of a birthright which had obvious economic potential (the Portuguese coffee settlers were doing quite well at the time) was politically explosive. As in the case of the Mau Mau in Kenya the popular force of the uprising tended to stay in ethnic and regional channels as local and ethnic symbolism gained dominance and the more urban and national political leadership failed to establish its own unity and effective national control. However, in Angola, unlike Kenya, rival leaderships with regional bases did make bids for national leadership and got foreign backing for their claims. The Popular Movement for the Liberation of Angola (MPLA) was the strongest, but when the National Union for the Total Independence of Angola (UNITA) and the National Front for the Liberation of Angola (FNLA) got support from South Africa, the United States, and Zaire; the MPLA called on the Soviet Union and Cuba for military assistance, which enabled them to consolidate their power (Davidson 1976). UNITA, with South African support, continued to harass the MPLA government militarily and to challenge its administrative grip in the south central region of the country.

If armed struggle does not readily overcome the forces of regionalism, what are its effects upon relations of leaders and masses, particularly peasant farmers? PAIGC, FRELIMO, and MPLA established liberated areas before they gained national power. They tried with some success to establish participatory and egalitarian political practices in the rural areas they controlled. Village committees, schools, medical posts, people's stores, and collective fields engaged political cadres, local citizens and fighting forces in common activities. Amilcar Cabral was acutely conscious of the split between government officials and people elsewhere in Africa and he wanted to take advantage of the special context of guerrilla war to build an egalitarian foundation for post-independence politics. He spoke of the advantages of having no permanent capital city where the official class would consolidate a privileged way of life. Instead he proposed that the government should move from region to region and thereby stay close to the needs and interests of ordinary people (Davidson 1969, 136–138).

In none of the colonies where nationalists won power in armed struggles did they gradually build an alternative state throughout the country. In Guinea-Bissau the process went some distance, but Cabral was murdered before the PAIGC succeeded to state power. The new government was quickly caught up in the issue of relations between the mainland and the Cabo Verde Island and the problems of governing the city and managing the economy. In Mozambique, FRELIMO had the strength and resolve to take power when Portugal's colonialist government was overthrown, but it had little organized presence in the southern part of the country where people and economic power were disproportionately concentrated. The MPLA's victory in Angola was based on its strength in and near Luanda. It had not had the time to build up a really dense governing structure in the rural areas where it was active. The abruptness of the transition to power; the overwhelming economic, administrative, and military issues faced; and the limitations of the political structures of liberated areas all reduced the longer-term impact of rural guerrilla warfare on the politics of peasant farming in the countries undergoing armed struggle for independence. However, the legacy of people's power may not be entirely played out.

The great political success of the leaderships which won the electoral and guerrilla struggles was the assumption of political power in legally sovereign nation states. In the succeeding decades many countries have had several transitions of government and most have passed power to another generation of leaders. Peasant farming, however, has remained a political problem. The qualities of peasant farming are related to such fundamental issues as political breakdown, weak government, and urban bias. From the point of view of the needs of peasant farmers, the problems of politics have been some combination of the limited nature of the dialogue they can engage in with government, the occurrence of repression and how to resist it, and, in extreme situations, how to survive as peasant farmers or even how to survive at all. The next chapter looks into these issues and problems.

§ 8 §

PEASANT FARMERS AS CITIZENS

The strength of the political voice of peasant farmers in Africa is a function of their social–economic position and of the way government and politics are structured. Many African governments passed through a phase of populist expansion of participation as aspiring national parties and leaders sought a popular following in the transition to independence. There frequently followed a period of growing centralization of political and economic control and shrinking opportunity for mass participation as single-party states were installed. As political parties have atrophied or been cancelled by no-party military regimes, observers have looked to patron–client relations, factional alignments, and personal followings for the link between rulers and the ruled in Africa (Sandbrook 1985). There still are variations in the structure of politics and government which are of particular importance for peasant farmers: existence of any kind of representative bodies (cooperatives, local councils, party committees, and popular committees); militarization of regional and local administration (use of armed services and the role of armed gangs); and the degree to which power is personalized. The influence of peasant farmers is one reason often given for the neo-patrimonial style of politics (in which personal power and patron–client relationships play a large role) thought to be typical of Africa. We will examine the question of how peasant farmers affect the overall style of politics after first considering the social basis of their power.

The political power of peasant farmers is grounded in their three-fold productive activity as producers for national and international markets, as self-provisioners, and sometimes as sellers or buyers of labour. It is shaped by their forms of organization and their guiding and motivating ideas. Finally, it is affected by the kinds of alliances, particularly the class alliances, whether explicit or implicit, which they form with other social sectors. After considering the bases of the political power of peasant farmers, the chapter will turn to the question of their overall political impact.

MARKET BARGAINING

The market relationship is central to the political strength and weakness of peasant farmers. Even where direct political competition has been eliminated and the government has no need to court voters, peasant farmers hold a vital bargaining chip, one which gains in value as governments are pressured by their international creditors to increase export earnings. As producers of exports which earn foreign exchange and of food and fibre for important domestic markets, peasant farmers have the potential of increasing or diminishing essential economic resources which directly affect government revenue. On one side their bargaining power depends upon how much the government needs their production. The potential power is greater for producers of crops which are major foreign exchange earners than it is for producers of minor crops for peripheral markets. On the other side, the degree to which the peasant farmers need the market also affects their bargaining power. What are their alternatives? If they can retreat into self-sufficiency, shift to other marketed crops, switch to alternative marketing channels, or move easily into wage labour, their bargaining position is much enhanced. Peasant farmers themselves have only limited control over the existence of strategic market options. They often strive to retain separate control over the self-provisioning alternative in order to reduce their vulnerability to markets. They lose that option as pressures on land, labour, and environment limit what they can produce.

The two peasant farming units described in chapter 3 had retained different sets of options. The Tanzania coffee grower, like many others in the region, had maintained a strong base of self-provisioning and had also invested heavily in the education of the children of the production unit in the hopes of qualifying them for salaried work. The Senegalese peanut producer had achieved a small foothold in retail trade as a supplement to selling the major cash crop. Neither of these peasant farmers had a real alternative to the major cash crop. In Senegal there had been some experimentation with cotton growing and even passing efforts to promote tomatoes for a tomato paste factory that never functioned. In Tanzania's southwestern highlands there were vague plans to diversify agriculture along the new road and rail lines linking Dar es Salaam to the Zambian copperbelt. But in neither region did the potential for alternative cash crops bear fruit. However, in the southern part of Senegal's peanut zone, marketing the crop through illegal parallel markets exporting through Gambia was a viable choice. In the years just before the government marketing organization was disbanded in 1980, the parallel network, with alleged clandestine backing from within the Islamic brotherhoods and within the state itself, carried a large fraction of the crop.

In the 1970s the Muslim brotherhoods had helped to

coordinate and amplify a 'revolt against the peanut' by recommending that producers look first to feeding their families and only second to paying their debts to cooperatives. Although the area planted to peanuts declined only very marginally, the government was shocked into raising the producer price significantly and into ceasing the unpopular practice of paying for peanuts with chits rather than with cash. It even forgave unpaid debts. Before the 1983 elections and again before the 1988 elections the official peanut price was even pushed above the world market price less marketing expenses. Although these were cases of successful market bargaining by Senegal's peanut growers abetted by Muslim brotherhoods which have been likened to trade unions (Cruise O'Brien 1979), it must be added that inflation has always rapidly eroded real gains in pricing and that the rural-to-urban terms of trade, at least until the IMF agreement of the mid 1980s, remained unfavourable to peanut producers.

Bargaining need not be organized or collective. Producers can exercise their economic power through their individual responses to similar price signals by abandoning the cash crop or switching marketing channels. If the government sees a slide in production or official marketing, it may raise prices or make marketing easier or cheaper by, for example, adding marketing points, paying more promptly, or improving farm-to-market roads. The flexibility of the government's response is limited by world market prices and, perhaps, by conditions imposed by international creditors. Such actions are conventionally seen as economic bargaining; buyer and seller are simply seeking their economic advantage and eventually they arrive at a market-clearing price. Note, however, that the existence or the absence of alternative cash crops and of alternative marketing channels is the consequence of social and political action by the government and by the rural population.

Government, producers, and intermediary groups of transporters and marketers have all frequently taken direct political action to shape the marketing relationship to better meet their needs. On the government side a major motive for creating or maintaining marketing boards in independent Africa has been the drive of the state to employ the power of a monopoly to strengthen its mastery over producers of vital commodities. Like the colonial trading companies and the colonial governments, the post-colonial leadership wanted to keep the upper hand in its economic relationship with peasant farmers. Evidence on pricing suggests that governments have frequently been successful in taxing away a high proportion, often on the order of 50 per cent, of the world market value of the major export crop (World Bank 1981, 56).

Chapter 5 described the structural disadvantage of the peasant farmers in the marketing relationship. They are numerous, scattered, and preoccupied with farming activities, while the marketing agencies are singular or few, concentrated, and professionally organized for purchasing. Nonetheless, peasant farmers have often supported the creation of marketing cooperatives or of parallel marketing channels in the form of routes for smuggling crops across borders. They have sought out and begun planting alternative cash crops and they have created or supported links to urban food markets. Peasant farmers are not entirely helpless in economic bargaining with buyers, even when the buyer is a government marketing board.

The arabica coffee growers of east-central Uganda were particularly adept organizers for bargaining about the conditions of marketing their highly valuable crop. They established a marketing cooperative and by dint of astute leadership and persistence won the right to sell their crop directly to external buyers. They saw the relations between coffee earnings, taxation levels, transportation costs, provision of pulping plants, maintenance of roads, and other government services. Their bargaining with the government reached beyond marketing itself to these other material relationships. The marketing cooperative became a multipurpose economic and political organization for the growers. After the Amin coup and the breakdown of government organization, the coffee growers turned their energies to production of food crops for themselves and for nearby markets. They were still able to market a portion of their crop over the border in Kenya and to buy goods there which were impossible to get in Uganda. The parallel market was a survival measure, not a bargaining tactic. Once the official market had broken down and coffee output had declined due to neglect of the trees, the producers had lost their bargaining leverage and politics gave way to coercion, violent clashes, and fearful manoeuvres to survive (Bunker 1987).

There are other examples of the breakdown of a relatively orderly and productive politics of explicit or implicit bargaining around the marketing relationship. For producers of export crops caught in the sphere of activity of a predatory political class whose factions fight among themselves, the reaction is to maximize self-reliance, to buy protection where possible, and to try to organize an alternative route for exports and purchases of essential goods. The capacity of peasant farmers to adapt to exploitation and to sustain an economy (even if it is one that falls far short of meeting basic material needs), helps to explain how a predatory system has survived for long periods in parts of Zaire.

Another kind of breakdown of peasant-farmer commodity production occurred in Ghana. Overtaxed and underserviced, cocoa production declined 'from a peak of

566,000 metric tons in 1965 to 249,000 tons in 1979', as farmers neglected their trees and failed to harvest their crop (World Bank 1981, 26). Where Ghana was different from Zaire or Uganda was in the relative absence of predation. The politics of bargaining was replaced not by a politics of violence and coercion, but by a combination of withdrawal and parallel action. The parallel activities were the familiar ones of marketing illegally across borders and selling food crops on urban markets. Withdrawal took the form of enlarging self-provisioning through food crop cultivation as well as by expanding hunting and gathering. Crafts were revived to provide non-agricultural consumer goods. Villagers saw to it that schooling continued and even expanded. In at least one village there is evidence that income rose with the successful pursuit of local self-reliance. Depending on the region the strategy of self-reliance was pursued in the name of regional, ethnic, or local loyalty and autonomy. There was a conscious sense of creating a community in opposition to the state or at least outside its range of control (Chazan 1983, 197–198).

In Mozambique the flight of the Portuguese population meant the dismantling of the rural trade network which served the peasant farmers and the worker-peasants. In itself, that was cause for a severe plight for peasant farmers. In addition the FRELIMO government decided initially to place almost all its agricultural development investment into the formation of very productive and modern irrigated state farms in the lower Limpopo valley north of Maputo, the capital city and largest market for foodstuffs. The policy was a twofold disaster: it failed to supply the marketing system, inputs, and consumer goods vital to the peasant farming sectors; and it failed to develop irrigated production to meet the urgent and rising food needs of the cities. Two other elements contributed to the resulting tragic scenario. One was a series of climatic catastrophes: droughts and floods which wiped out harvests, crops, and water control systems vital to the rural economy. The final disastrous element was the sponsorship by South Africa of a military force gathered from among former agents of the Portuguese secret police. That force, the Mozambique National Resistance (MNR), has systematically attacked the lifelines of the rural economy. Faced with a desperate economic and military situation, the government since 1983 has shifted its agricultural policy sharply towards 'capitalist and family agriculture' (Roesch 1988, 73).

Another extreme form of the market relationship is found where government tries to prevent bargaining completely by requisitioning crops or commanding cultivation of a given hectarage of the crop. The Central African Republic has forced peasant farmers to grow cotton, and Amin's government in Uganda required coffee to be delivered for sale against the will of the growers. Here is where silent forms of resistance can come into play. The cotton may be neglected; perhaps the seeds will fail to sprout. The coffee somehow is not properly dried. Political dialogue has given way to domination and resistance. Where some element of bargaining is still alive, the politics can still be tough and conflictual. Tax and credit payment requirements may make the delivery of a certain amount of the cash crop virtually compulsory for most farmers. Alternative marketing channels may be closed down or harassed. Markets and support for alternative crops may not be provided. Peasant farmers may organize to refuse to market their crops or to repay loans to official credit agencies. They may demonstrate against local authorities identified with the prices they consider unfair. They may even attack the offices of local administration and of marketing.

If in Ghana much space was left for local political and economic creative reaction to breakdown of the main market relationship between peasant farmers and the state, and if in Uganda the economic and political bargain was replaced by a struggle marked by armed clashes and coercive invasions, in Mozambique the MNR engages in systematic destruction and terror designed to eliminate and poison all the points of productive contact between state agencies and peasant farmers. Marketing points, schools, social service projects, transportation links, medical posts, and crop storage depots are all chosen targets for material destruction and for striking fear and despair into the hearts of rural people. Here is an anti-politics of peasant farming carried out by neither peasant farmers nor by the state, but by an externally supported force. Out of the destruction comes famine and depopulation as peasant farmers seek sustenance and security elsewhere.

Political action has an indirect effect upon the economic bargain by structuring the alternatives. The cases of breakdown reveal one of the boundaries of the politics of market bargaining. They reveal that there can be a productive political element even in the unequal exchange between peasant farmers and governments. They also reveal that peasant farmers have some capacity for protecting themselves against predation and neglect. The case of the MNR's wholly destructive strategy in Mozambique marks the absolute limits of economic breakdown, the wholesale destruction of peasant farming. The violent, but far from total, breakdown of east-central Uganda and the less violent and more constructive breakdown in Ghana reveal the defensive and the creative political capacities of some peasant-farming communities.

POLITICAL BELIEFS

The language of material interests is just one of the languages spoken by peasant farmers in the political dialogues in which they engage. It is the language in which compromise is easiest since there is room for give and take with respect to prices and investments by interests on all sides of the discussion. The language of money favours the leadership of larger-scale producers, traders, and transporters within the rural community; these are the interests most closely tied to the system of marketing and the government activities which support marketing. The governments of Côte d'Ivoire and Kenya have encouraged peasant farmers to talk and think in the language of material interest. Striving to improve one's income is held out as a laudable goal. In some form material interests enter the political vocabulary of all peasant-farming communities, but there are important variations in the broader language of peasant-farming politics.

One area of difference is in the dominant idea of justice. Research on peasant farmers in Southeast Asia has discovered that they have a strong sense of their right to a culturally defined minimum subsistence income which governments and traders ought not to infringe. Taxation or profit-taking which does not violate the subsistence minimum will not offend the popular sense of justice nearly as strongly as violations of the subsistence minimum will (Scott 1976). The Muslim leaders of Senegal who recommended that their followers look to meeting their family needs before consenting to pay debts duly contracted with the government were expressing a similar idea of justice. It is probable that peasant farmers elsewhere in Africa cling strongly to their right to have their essential minimum income protected from violation by more powerful classes and institutions. It is also probable that the subsistence ethic, as it has been called, is weakened where wage labour and wide inequality have been incorporated into the peasant farming society. The wider variety of ways to meet basic needs probably goes along with an idea of justice centred on the right to a job and the right to a fair return to labour. The obligation to fulfill these rights is likely to be assigned to government and to locally powerful patrons. Often the sense of having such rights will be tempered by recognition that peasant farmers are economically and politically weak.

The attitude to inequality also varies greatly in peasant farming communities. Many of Africa's rural societies have long traditions of great social equality, an attitude given material backing by open access to land. In such societies, especially in the early stages of cash-crop expansion, there may be resentment against those farmers who become strikingly more wealthy than others. In the southwestern coffee region of Tanzania there were incidents in which expanding coffee farmers found their coffee trees cut down by worried and perhaps resentful neighbours. In another district of the same region of Tanzania more prosperous farmers who were believed to have colluded with government authorities for their advantages were often the targets of witchcraft and other social sanctions (Van Hekken and Van Velsen 1972). A belief in equality also may colour the view of peasant farmers about their representatives to cental government. Again in Tanzania survey research during the 1970 general election found that peasant farmers frequently voted against incumbent members of parliament on the grounds that they had now had 'their chance to eat' in Dar es Salaam and had lost touch with their home community. It was time to give the opportunity of urban experience and wealth to someone else who was still connected with the rural community (Moris 1974, 350–351).

Other African peasant-farming communities incorporate acceptance of social and economic inequality. In Senegal the old distinctions between nobles, freeborn, and slaves and between certain endogamous castes and other people still influences attitudes to their descendants. The spiritual ascendency of the families of the great religious leaders is also accepted. In Senegal one can speak of a peasant-farmer aristocracy while recognizing that it has multiple origins and a certain fluidity, but is backed by widely held acceptance of a rural political and social status hierarchy. In many peasant-farming regions chiefly families retained their claim to superior dignity even while they used their access to land and government assistance to take the lead in cash crop production. Where chiefly status was incorporated into the colonial state structure and maintained by the independent governments, as in Northern Nigeria and in Uganda, or where social and economic inequalities became imbedded in accepted religious and political institutions, as with the Islamic societies of Senegal and Sudan, popular political thinking tends to accept the existence of a pyramid of power extending from a peasant-farming village through headmen and religious or chiefly leaders into regional and national structures of power. More egalitarian communities may tend to see the whole local rural community as an egalitarian social unit subject to the authority and intervention of outsiders. Here, as in many other areas of political belief, is a topic for much more research by scholars with the appropriate cultural sensitivities and skills.

Issues of distributive justice can become active political issues in peasant-farming societies. Where the productive core of shared material interests still unites peasant farmers with government through the marketing and service-providing relationships, the question of fairness of prices and taxes can always be raised. Different peasant-farming communities respond differently to claims about fairness, depending upon how strongly they adhere to the right to a minimum livelihood and how egalitarian their sentiments are. In principle, however, these issues are subject to bargaining and compromise, at least until the threshold of a minimum livelihood is crossed. However, the political expression of peasant-farming communities extends beyond questions of material interests and economic justice to include other interests, some of them less tractable to compromise and some of them extremely useful vehicles for political mobilization (Beer and Williams 1974).

The symbol of peasant-farmer unity against central economic and political institutions is likely to be a regional or ethnic one rather than one identifying peasant farmers only. The reason for this is that the organizing cadres of the region are likely to be traders, chiefs, religious leaders, or local administrators who are linked by interest and position to the peasant-farming economy. In east-central Uganda, the ideology of the coffee farmers combined an affirmation of Bagisu ethnic dignity, a demand for fair coffee prices and local control of profits, and the claim of managerial efficiency in coffee marketing. The ethnic identification and local definition of issues stood in the way of nationwide organization of common peasant-farmer interests (Bunker 1987, 187–191). In Ghana under Nkrumah, issues concerning the marketing and pricing of cocoa were expressed in terms of Asante ethnic regionalism and brought the country to independence with its political unity seriously challenged (Genoud 1969, 70).

The changing nature of Africa's peasant-farming communities raises issues much wider than those of farmer income and the definition of community boundaries. Rural communities all over sub-Saharan Africa have learned of the benefits of schooling, medical attention, clean water, and good roads. Desire for improvements in these government services often unites peasant-farming communities in political action. The *harambee* movement in Kenya mobilizes local leaders and followers around community development projects which symbolize local support for the government and for a locally-based representative, and at the same time claim material resources from the central government. As the government has become more repressive, the balance has shifted from extraction of central resources by the locality to expression of loyalty to the centre by the locality. The loyalty also symbolizes acquiescence in the direction of development pursued by the government. Similar actions in many countries, even if less elaborate, equally demonstrate loyalty, support, enterprise, and a claim for investment of government resources in the locality (Holmquist 1984).

The Tanzanian leadership put forward an official development ideology designed to legitimize a direction of change for the nation's peasant-farming communities. In the Arusha Declaration of 1965 Nyerere proclaimed the objective of socialist rural production. Ironically, the result was fifteen years of confusion and uncertainty about what aspects of peasant farming were legitimate. Many of the ideas of rural socialism and self-reliance struck a positive chord with many peasant farmers: stress on self-reliance, equality, and help among kin and neighbours. However, the strictures against the hiring of labour and the frowning upon private trade set the government against the large farmers and expanding operators in the most economically dynamic regions. These people were recognized as leaders by many smaller peasant farmers. The disbanding of the cooperative societies in 1976 marginalized the regional leadership which had used cooperatives as its base for economic expansion and political influence, favouring in many cases the larger producers, but not rejected by smaller-scale farmers (Coulson 1982, 278). The close control of political discussion by the national single party prevented an alternative ideology from appearing. Instead there were efforts to stress the most acceptable parts of ujamaa: cooperation and self-help in the creation of community services, cooperation and even collective labour in the founding of new settlements, and collective appeal for government support. There was also a great deal of hypocrisy and action under false pretences. Officials who knew that ujamaa was not a practical guide to peasant farming or to its realistic transformation nonetheless often collaborated in the charade. For them, however, it had the merit of justifying the presence and the actions of central officials and technicians of economic development and socialism.

As an ideological initiative to draw peasant farmers into a productive national political dialogue, ujamaa in Tanzania must be judged a failure. However, it has the distinction of being one of the few serious attempts to construct a consistent language for the developmental politics of peasant farming. Within its framework an effort was made to address some of the divisive issues of changing production. Chapter 6 discussed some of the divisions typical of changing peasant-farming communities: bigger producers versus smaller ones; different ethnic groups; generational and sexual divisions; peasant farmers versus traders versus administrators; religious differences. How will changes in production and in productivity affect the different groups? Which groups will get most from government services? Rural credit and extension services are frequently seen to benefit larger farmers first and foremost. New crops and new forms of production such as using animal-drawn equipment will make some farmers more productive and richer. They may impoverish other farmers. One community or region may gain big advantages over other communities or regions. Women may be disadvantaged. On the whole the ideology of ujamaa came down on the side of equality. The government attempted not to give preference to richer agricultural regions in the supply of services, even if they supplied most of the foreign exchange vital to the investment programme. In the period before forced villagization, however, the government did give preference in the provision of services to ujamaa villages which claimed to adhere to the principles of living and working together for the good of all.

Little has been published about the way in which members of ujamaa villages discussed and resolved the issues of changing social and production relations. They favoured sharing out income according to the amount of work each member contributed to collective activities. But the accounts give scant attention to the issues of family property; the sexual division of labour; relations among elders, adults, and youth; the preferred priority of public services; how to cope with cultural differences; how to handle conflict; how to deal with differences in talent. We know almost nothing about the terms in which such issues are discussed or whether Nyerere's writings on ujamaa became a practical guide.

Ujamaa attempted to face some of the important issues. More common has been an unreflective championing of the values of capitalist modernization. Peasant farmers are lauded as the salt of the earth and instructed to improve their productivity. They are asked to support the government in return for the social services which the government provides, even while those services may be disintegrating. Frequently government promises of better farmgate prices and new investments in the countryside are followed by declining prices and investment which benefit only a few peasant farmers. The language of modernization may give those peasant farmers who are doing well the words to justify their success, but it does not have an idiom for discussing the painful issues of inequality and social conflict which the process of change brings.

Changes in government role and in relations within communities generate fundamental questions: What kind of community shall we create? Perhaps more volatile and pressing: What kinds of rural community will be discarded? Small movements of spiritual defense and renewal are common in rural Africa. Some of them represent those groups which are losing out in the process of social change. They want to revive the ideas and conditions of better days. The more complex tensions noted above may also find local political expression and may even flow into a wider stream of social and cultural awakening. Endeavours to recapture lost worlds can take on ethnic and religious colours and extend beyond peasant farmers to become regional movements. However, for peasant farming regions in which production for the market is well established, the ideology of fair prices, adequate government services, and some room for local management is likely to form a core belief. Peasant farmers are unlikely to abandon their economic interests even as they join in wider movements.

Beyond that core of ideas the language of politics needs ways of discussing and resolving the many issues which change is bringing. Key people in the process of creation of political language, a process which is far too little known in academic writing, are local political leaders. They are often seen as power brokers and gatekeepers; their work as language brokers is seldom noticed. They translate between the language of national policy and the local idiom of politics. Often the translation is literal: from French to Tukolor, from Swahili to Kinyiha. Always there is a disparity of ideas, conceptions, goals, and issues to work on and to work with. It makes a great difference whether the political translators are religious leaders, traders, party cadres, larger farmers, chiefs, or representative villagers of a variety of backgrounds. Understanding better the process of ideological translation between peasant-farming communities and the government is a great need of social science. Strengthening the process itself is a great political need in rural Africa.

ORGANIZATION

For leaders and leading ideas to give direction to political movements and conflicts in rural Africa, they require the assistance of organization. Chapter 7 presented the repertoire of precolonial African forms of organization and discussed how they were used and transformed in the political movements for independence. Peasant farming continues to be ordered by kinship and clanship as well as by marketing and administration. Specifically political organizations have to take account of the pre-existing forms of organization which are part of everyday life in peasant-farming regions. Either they build on existing social organization or they fight against it.

Since independence one trend in political organization has been the withering and dismantling of mass party organization. Where they live on, parties have usually become shadowy symbols of support for the government rather than viable structures for doing political work with peasant-farming communities. Competitive elections in Senegal, Botswana, and Nigeria and semi-competitive ones elsewhere have given periodic life to political parties. In Ghana under Jerry Rawlings' second government and in Burkina Faso under Thomas Sankoré popular organization reappeared for a brief time. In Ghana the popular committees were few and weak in the peasant-farming areas (Hansen 1987). The exceptions further reveal the weakness of party organization in rural Africa. Some academic writing at the time of independence forecast a powerful continuing role for political parties on the grounds that they were the authentic creation of social traditions and the expression of social needs under a strong new form of leadership. In fact they had been an expression of the need of the new nationalist political class for mass electoral support. Once that need was past, the organization fell by the wayside.

In Senegal, partly because of the competitive elections, the ruling Parti Socialist has kept in touch with its grass roots. During the 1983 general election I observed how hard one member of the National Assembly from the peanut region worked to mend his relations with all parts of his district. He had to see to it that the villages and groups which felt the most neglected had a promise of new wells, roads, and schools. He also had to work at repairing the patron–client network and resolving conflicts at more local levels of political organization. The complexities of peasant-farming regions give plenty of opportunity for conflicts to surface. Politically speaking, local party officials and leaders have to run hard to keep the social power structure in the same place.

A few governments tried to bypass old and build new forms of organization for peasant farmers and for other sectors of the population, which would serve the needs of development. Tanzania again stands out for the self-conscious effort of its leadership to reshape the political party and the administration into organizational tools for social and economic development. At the grass roots of party organization was the ten-house cell. Each ten households, roughly speaking, were to form a cell of the Tanganyika African National Union and later the Chama Cha Mapinduzi (CCM). In 1970 the structure was reliable enough to be taken as the framework for selecting and finding a random sample of those eligible to vote in peasant farming districts. Every citizen could in principle trace his or her party linkage up through local, district, and regional committees to the national council of the party and the party president, Julius Nyerere. Local party cells and committees played a role in the resolution of local disputes and elections of representatives to higher party councils (Election Study Committee 1974).

In the 1970s the leadership tried to make the party a stronger intermediary between national leaders and local communities. In its national party school in Dar es Salaam and in several regional schools it gave special training to its regional and district cadres. The cadres were meant to play an active role in villages and district and regional development committees, reaching into peasant-farming communities and influencing their development projects (Mwansasu 1979).

The hand of party cadres and government administrators was strengthened by the policy of villagization carried out in the mid 1970s. The government moved a large portion of the rural population, perhaps 5 million people, from scattered homesteads into agglomerated settlements. Those who declined to move were forced to comply. The government did not require collective production, but it did establish a stronger administrative and political presence in many villages (Coulson 1982, 235–262).

Villagization is not unique to Tanzania. In the mid 1980s Ethiopia moved 4.5 million peasant farmers from the arid north into new settlements in the fertile southwest and also embarked on a programme to relocate scattered homesteads into concentrated villages (Africa News 1987, 6). Many other governments have encouraged new settlement along roads and near marketing points. Even in the absence of government pressure, there is much spontaneous movement to get closer to transportation and services. Both spontaneous and mandatory villagization strengthen the links between peasant farming communities and the centres of political and economic power. As yet we know very little about the effect of villagization on the way peasant farmers organize themselves, represent their own interests, and think about what their interests are. It is plausible to argue that peasant farmers in organized villages will have stronger and wider interests in social services; that the hand of younger, school-educated, and wealthier intermediaries will be enhanced; and that the ability of peasant farmers to formulate and express political interests will be strengthened.

An even more thorough form of social and political organization imposed from above has been the numerous but widely scattered integrated rural development schemes favoured by the World Bank and other international lenders in the 1970s. In a cotton scheme in Burkina Faso, settlement pattern, house design, and pattern of work were all designated by the scheme (Gervais 1984). In Zambia similar controls were exercised, although some representation from scheme members was built into the scheme (Ray 1979). In Nigeria the controls of some of the schemes are much looser and directed mainly to the larger producers (Dunmoye 1986). The limit is probably reached with the sugar schemes in Kenya, where the members sign contracts with the scheme management, setting out in great detail the work of the members. If a member fails to fulfill a certain action, the scheme management has the right to send in a team to do the job and to charge the member's account for the work done (Hansen and Marcussen 1982).

Politically, members of schemes tend to become 'state peasantries' dependent upon the government for an economic position which promises the advantage of a higher and more secure income. Economic controls may in fact prescribe the work of all members of a household and it may be experienced as overbearing interference in family life. The controls have been particularly difficult for women to endure. In addition to the work assigned them by the scheme they have a large non-agricultural work load caring for children, preparing food, fetching wood and water, and maintaining the household. The political side of scheme organization, therefore, contains cross-cutting pressures. Members may feel privileged and exploited at the same time. Some schemes give a certain leverage to members who may be able to threaten withdrawal of labour at crucial moments. The skills they learn may make members difficult to replace. There is room for much more research on the political organization and action of members of villages and of integrated rural development schemes.

Women and youth in peasant farming regions often have special needs and interests. Dependence of youth on their elders for land and for assistance in marrying creates tensions. Their higher level of schooling than the elders gives them skills, opportunities, and ideas that their elders cannot share. Women, too, are in a special position because of the sexual division of labour in much farm work, because of the inferior legal and social status usually assigned to them, and because of the restricted opportunity they have for education and for employment outside farm and household. It is therefore not surprising to find special youth organizations and women's organizations in rural areas of Africa. Most often such organizations function to control their members and to channel their actions in directions which preserve existing power relations, but occasionally special group organizations will make strong claims in the interests of their members.

Locally-based organizations of social and political power are of special importance for the self-organization of rural communities that withdraw, by choice or by force of circumstance, from the power of central institutions. Clan and kinship organization take on a more fully political function. Old leadership roles such as that of spirit medium may revive and flourish, sometimes in conjunction with political leadership by revolutionary cadres (Ranger 1985; Lan 1985). Where power has broken up among armed groups, armed gangs may become the new local intermediaries with external powers, to the detriment of stable cultivation and regular marketing. The effects upon peasant farming can be devastating, as the diverse experiences of Uganda, southern Sudan, and Mozambique have shown (Bunker 1987; Cammack 1987).

The examples of peasant-farming communities where the wide political system has broken down serve to underline the impact of central organization and of the explicit and implicit alliances peasant farmers form with other groups.

ALLIANCES

Although they are the largest major economic group in most African countries, peasant farmers are but one of many sources of pressure, interest, ideas, revenue, and difficulty with which governments must deal. Any consideration of the politics of peasant farmers needs to give attention to their place in the wider political process. Other groups may be the basis of support or opposition to peasant farming interests and ideas. There are conflicting views about what are the natural or possible coalitions of forces which might assemble to support a government and a policy.

Interest clusters

Among the other major interest clusters are foreign governments, international agencies, and multinational businesses. Whatever their specific interests, as a group they stand for openness to foreign investment, maintenance of debt repayments, and continuing supply of major exports. Chapter 5 showed how they generally favour policies which strengthen the market orientation and economic productivity and stability of peasant farming. The ideological framework of much international advice and pressure in the late 1980s is privatization, market rationality, and anticommunism.

The urban-based groups with which government decision-makers must contend include the state apparatus itself, whose members defend their jobs and functions; a sector of national private business seeking to expand against or in partnership with government and foreign business (in some cases this group can be divided into businesses closely tied to foreign trade and investment and businesses aiming to develop production in the country); workers in the formal sector who are often unionized; the vast informal sector of small traders and artisans with semi-wage labour; and the unemployed who shade into the informal semi-employed. One view holds that there is an urban coalition that includes almost all of these groups, uniting them in favour of more urban services and subsidies for food and lodging. Workers, it is argued, can feel their basic consumption needs are being supported and employers can see that their wage payments are kept down. Policies designed to fill these urban needs mean low prices to farmers and less money for rural services – grounds, one might think, for the organization of an effective peasant-farmer political coalition (Bates 1981).

There are major barriers inhibiting formation of a broad rural or peasant-farming interest group. As was stressed in chapters 4 and 5, the sector is diverse. In addition to peasant farmers there may be large landholders, small and medium sized traders, government employees, rural wage-workers, sharecroppers, scheme tenants, pastoralists, religious leaders and other dignitaries. Peasant farmers themselves are divided by degree of market commitment, size of operation, wealth, crop, region, language group, and other factors. As the public choice perspective described in chapter 6 notes, divisions among peasant farmers, their geographical dispersal, their need to work on the land many months of the year, and the weakness of communications systems all raise the cost and the difficulty of political organization among peasant farmers.

The balance of organizational political power in favour of urban groups has been reinforced by the stifling of competitive political mobilization by the governing groups in Africa. They have eliminated competitive elections by establishing one-party states, or, in the case of many military governments, by outlawing or restricting all parties. Where the urban coalition needs rural allies it seeks them not with peasant farmers, but with the chiefly families, traders and transporters, large-scale producers, or participants in special intensive government schemes. It can give special subsidies and privileges to the rural elite while still biasing pricing and investment policies in favour of the urban coalition (Bates 1981).

Coalition of intermediaries

Looked at more closely, the urban coalition is not entirely urban and it does not include all elements of the urban population. Some kind of rural elite is usually favoured. The urban unemployed and semi-employed, some recently driven from farming, are only very marginally better off in the city than in the country. Even the better paid and unionized wage-labour force sees its real wages drop with falling export earnings and declining government spending; it is only tenuously part of a political coalition with a leadership it may challenge. This is one of the reasons for the weakness and instability of African governments. Perhaps the best description is 'coalition of intermediaries', since it is made up of the political and economic middle men and women, together with some capitalists who dominate the state.

Allies for peasant farmers

Several proposals have been made about the way the peasant-farming sector has achieved or might achieve a position of greater political strength. The proposals can be divided into upper-class coalitions, a peasant-farmer coalition with international capital, and lower-class coalitions.

It is argued that in Kenya the governing class of administrative, political, and business officials often invests in agricultural land. Ministers, principal secretaries, and factory owners own coffee, tea, and dairy farms in the central highlands. Those who did not inherit farms took advantage of the land redistribution schemes which Africanized ownership of large parts of the European-owned highlands and of the new freehold tenure to acquire farms. Wives and children of the urban elite may manage the farms. Unfortunately, there is little research to indicate the extent to which the urban elite is also an agrarian class, but that interest is offered as an explanation for the relatively more favourable agricultural pricing policy followed by the Kenya government and for the consequent impressive performance of Kenyan agriculture (Lofchie, forthcoming).

If in Kenya the urban elite bought farms, in Côte d'Ivoire, as explained in chapter 7, the owners and manager of larger cocoa and coffee farms were at the forefront of the political party that inherited power from the French colonial government. As noted already, the post-colonial government headed by the former president of the African planters association, Félix Houphouët-Boigny, was sympathetic to the interests of the peasant farming sector in marketing, pricing, employing farm labour, and providing inputs and infrastructure. Again, as in Kenya, the peasant farming sector has been unusually successful. There is energetic debate about whether the large-scale peasant farmers who work on their land and who employ labour at the same time qualify as a capitalist class distinct from the small-scale peasant farmers who employ little labour. There is also disagreement about whether rural capitalists or a bureaucratic class, some of whose members invest in farming as absentee landlords, have gained the upper hand in control of the state. All sides seem to agree that the early political influence of the peasant farmers lent a rural bias to the government's agricultural policy in its early years (Amin 1967; Campbell 1974 and 1978; Fauré and Médard 1982). Recent research claims that large-scale and small-scale cash crop farmers who work on their crops alongside their employees belong to a single peasant-farming class which is strongly divided from the state managers and from the agricultural entre- preneurs who invest in cocoa and coffee farms as absentee landlords (Faure and Médard 1982). However, govern- ment pricing has not squeezed the cocoa growers of Côte d'Ivoire as hard as Ghana's growers have been squeezed. Moreover, the controlled elections in the Côte d'Ivoire have not registered the discontent of the cocoa and coffee growers.

Benefits of an agrarian elite

More generally, the case is made that an agricultural elite, whether it be one evolving from rural or urban origins, can strengthen the political voice of the rural sector as a whole. Since small farmers as well as large benefit from good prices, good roads, and available inputs, small farmers need not find in large owners a class enemy. The relative equality of peasant farmers in Africa, by this argument, may be a weakness for the group as a whole. Without an elite with large economic interests at stake, good organizing capacity, connections in the world of urban power, and the influence of recognized social position the representatives of peasant farmers cannot make their interests felt (Bates 1981).

The idea of an upper-class urban–rural coalition may look attractive compared to the urban-centred policies which have failed to support African agriculture, but it has a troubling underside. First, there is the prospect that some rural areas or agricultural projects will be favoured to the neglect of others. All rural areas and the producers of all crops will not gain entry to the dominant coalition. The fate of the regions without export crops will not be improved by a partial rural–urban elite coalition. Second, many peasant-farming zones now contain different classes with distinct and possibly conflicting interests. In Côte d'Ivoire, as already explained, a large part of the agricultural labour force in the peasant-farming or capitalist-farming zone is made up of immigrants from Burkina Faso and northern regions of the country. Their living and working conditions are miserable compared to those of the owner elite. They benefit little, if at all, from the rural–urban coalition. Nor do the urban poor benefit, except from the few resources which may trickle down from the prosperity of the export market.

A 'triple alliance' for Africa?

Another, and at first glance unlikely, ally of peasant farming is sometimes indicated in the IMF and the World Bank, the active representatives of international finance capital in its relations with Africa. The idea is that international capital wants to maintain ample production of agricultural commodities like coffee, tea, cotton, sugar, sisal, pyrethrum, and groundnuts. Ample production means low prices, and the industries which process these raw materials and market the products benefit from the low prices. International lenders are more likely to get their service and principal payments from economies that are still earning foreign exchange. Peasant farmers will keep the goods and the repayments flowing without changing the international pattern of manufacturing or challenging the position of international capital. Thus the IMF and the World Bank support policies and governments which improve prices, training, inputs, and transportation for their peasant-farming sectors. International capital is pressing the urban-biased governing coalitions to do better by the peasant farmers (World Bank 1981; 1984; 1986).

What is shaping up as the most favoured strategy for African agricultural development is a special African form of the 'triple alliance', heralded as the coordinator of industrialization in Brazil and South Korea. The industrializing triple alliance consisted of multinational manufacturing capital, national manufacturing capital, and the state agreeing on a policy of investment and labour management from which all members of the alliance would benefit. In Africa, private international capital has minimal interest in African agriculture, but international finance capital wants to maintain the export economy. It seeks to find an ally in the business sector, either national or international, which will benefit from the marketing, transport, and input supply. It may also accept government into the alliance as long as it plays by market rules. The third member of the alliance is the peasant-farming class, defined as farmers with enough land and labour to expand with improved markets and technology. The agrarian triple alliance ignores the land-poor, the landless, and the peripheral regions. Some also see it as having the effect, intentional or not, of cutting Africa out of more fundamental and productive transformations of rural and urban economies. The crisis in African agriculture and the debt pressures on African government give enormous leverage to international finance to work toward the formation of such alliances.

A peasant–worker coalition?

The new triple alliance is put forward as an economically progressive replacement for the urban coalition of government, private business, urban wage-workers, and urban semi-employed which, it is claimed, has starved the rural sector of investment while taxing it into impoverishment (Lofchie 1986). Socialists, especially leaders of socialist governments have proposed another kind of alliance – a coalition of peasants and workers – as the basis for a government of the exploited for socially and economically progressive development. What are the prospects for such a coalition? The answer requires consideration of the divisions in both urban and rural sectors.

Peasant farmers who employ seasonal labour have conflicting interests on wage levels and access to land. The peasant farmers want low wages and a firm grip on the land; the rural workers want high wages and access to land of their own. Peasant farmers benefit from the high food prices which raise the cost of living of urban wage workers. In paying a high proportion of the world market price to the producers, a government denies itself tax revenue which could pay for urban investment. Thus peasants and urban workers find their immediate interests in conflict.

Developmental interests, however, could unite workers and peasant farmers. Rising peasant-farming production of food and exports means more foreign exchange for the whole economy. High prices to peasant farmers slows urban migration and reduces downward pressure on urban wages. Higher urban wages enlarge the market for peasant-farmer food production. To create the common developmental interests is the work of a government with some control over the economy. If investment is hostage to high debt service charges and if the income of rural and urban consumers is guided by world primary product markets subject to wild price fluctuations, then the prospect for uniting peasant farmers with workers is very dim. Even under favourable international economic conditions a political leadership would have to work hard to keep a worker–peasant alliance alive and active.

Under prevailing international economic conditions, constructing such an alliance would be particularly difficult. Within rural society the ties of social domination and isolation can be very strong. There is protection as well as exploitation in the way rural inequality functions. The socialist political parties which have seen peasants and workers as their class base, have so far failed to give urban workers or peasant farmers a strong and independent voice in the governing coalition. As the rural crisis deepens and rural class divisions intensify, at least in certain countries, the possibility of such an alliance may become stronger. In many parts of Africa, for the time being, a more realistic way of bringing the poor peasant farmers into the political equation is to create an opening for democratization within peasant-farming communities and to pressure those communities to heed the claims of the disadvantaged who are willing to speak up.

The question of political alternatives must raise at the same time questions of the restricted content of the dialogue between government and peasant farmers. Can peasant farmers express their real needs and interests? How can the political dialogue be widened?

WIDENING THE DIALOGUE

Government actions engage a wide range of issues concerning family and community relations as well as the more apparent economic interests of peasant farmers. Therefore, it is not surprising that peasant farmers have taken part in a wide variety of political actions. In addition to marketing boycotts and tax resistance there have been demands for schools, health clinics, and water systems. There have been complaints against the taking of land for big schemes and alterations in marketing and transport which add to the costs of peasant farmers. Religious bodies, women's organizations, youth clubs, and community associations express other claims and grievances in those places where there is some means of political dialogue. Conflicts over land, leadership, and inheritance reflect increasing pressures on the land and changing relations between husbands and wives, parents and children.

At the same time, within governments there are discussions among experts about changing price levels, reorganizing marketing, promoting new crops, establishing new high intensity agricultural schemes, increasing security of land title, promoting resettlement schemes, cutting the education budget, and increasing agricultural research. However, the two dialogues seldom intersect.

The marketing imperative ties peasant farmers and the state tightly together. The best and clearest opportunity for political dialogue centres on prices of crops and inputs, methods of marketing and supplying, and ways of improving production of existing crops on existing farms. The dialogue, even on these bread and butter (or grain and ghee) issues is deflected, very often, by the powerful political role of the local intermediaries whose interests only partially correspond with those of the peasant farmers. Furthermore, the basic economic issues bring in their train a set of more complex social issues. The change in the marketing relationship ramifies onto the self-provisioning and wage-labour circuits of relationships. Within the community the relative standing and opportunity of larger peasant farmers and smaller ones may be at stake.

To the extent that a government is able to assist peasant farmers to adopt tools and methods which increase production, it will also face the indirect issues of change. Even without change in productivity, the strains and stresses of social relations in peasant-farming communities create potential political issues. Many of them can be solved within the community, but if the national dialogue of rural politics is to become healthier, governments will need to broaden the dialogue on rural change.

§ 9 §

CRISIS AND OPPORTUNITY

There is no doubt that peasant farming in Africa will continue to face grave crises in the near future. It can be anticipated that large regions in the drought-prone areas of the Sahel zone and the drier farming areas south of the equator will in some years experience further crop failure. In these and other areas the rising population and increasing area of land that each peasant farmer can cultivate will push the intensity of land use to a level which results in a downward slide of diminishing returns and ecological damage. The Sahara will continue to expand. Smaller disasters of flooding and localized crop failures will also continue to occur.

At the same time there are huge areas of rural Africa which have not suffered an agricultural crisis. In these regions and even in regions experiencing economic and political insecurity peasant farmers have resources and means for self-protective action. There are two difficult questions: How can regions and groups facing grave crises be helped to avoid the worst? And how can regions of stronger peasant farming find a route to increasing production and improved standard of living?

LEARNING FROM DISASTERS

Peasant farmers often have the capacity to withstand difficult years. Their mixture of crops and multiple sources of income, their kinship ties and community links of mutual support, and their food reserves and borrowing capacity can often see them through a bad spell. But when ecological damage is widespread, when community safety nets collapse, and when market institutions break down, peasant farmers become extremely vulnerable. They have to rely on the government to channel and coordinate help. Considering the circumstances of the breakdown of peasant farming is one route to understanding the minimum requirements for the health of peasant-farming communities.

Basic security

The most destructive disasters for peasant-farming zones in Africa have been cases of political as well as economic breakdown. In Ethiopia the government of Hailie Selassie set an example of political callousness and administrative incompetence for a large region of peasant farming when in 1973–74 his government ignored and suppressed information about a building crisis of starvation in which hundreds of thousands of people died and a large region's economy was devastated. Unfortunately the succeeding military government claiming a Marxist direction is guilty of a repetition of the same criminal combination of inaction and suppression at a cost of more hundreds of thousands of lives. It is hard to imagine a more complete severing of government policy from peasant-farming interests. In these cases, as well as in the cases of starvation in secessionist Biafra during Nigeria's civil war (where two million died) and hunger and starvation in Uganda during the Amin period, government had not only broken down, but was at war with a region. Destroying a peasantry and killing the seeming supporters of the enemy became a policy for some government officials or, at best, an unavoidable consequence of war.

The efforts of South Africa to weaken and starve the

peasant farming regions of Mozambique are appallingly effective. The government of South Africa supports the actions of the MNR to destroy rural trade and government services and to demoralize community leaders and development officials, and it reduces access to wage labour on the part of Mozambique's peasant-workers. Presumably the leaders of South Africa's white government think they are attacking an example of revolutionary government and a potential source of support for majority claims to political rights in South Africa. Those who suffer most directly, in addition to the people who are killed, are the millions of peasant farmers whose ability to feed and support themselves is undermined or destroyed. Moreover, the government's capacity to get help to the suffering is severely reduced by South Africa's attacks. The collapse of the colonial economic pattern when the Portuguese settlers fled and the large-scheme policies of the Mozambique government during the first decade of independence weakened the peasant-farming sector and made the South African task easier. But the tragedy of the late 1980s is that the rulers of South Africa are preventing a willing and able government from getting assistance to its own people.

Security is the first precondition of a healthy peasant farming sector. A minimum of peace and order, allowing crops to move out and consumer goods to move in, encouraging local trade, and permitting circulation of labour is an essential requirement. Although the regions of insecurity are extensive, most of rural Africa and most of Africa's peasant farmers have the basic security upon which more productive policies may be built.

Environmental health
An environmental crisis (often the consequence of years of inappropriate economic policy) can undermine peasant

farming even where security is adequate. In the Sahel drought and the western Sudan famine security was not an issue, but the calibre of the economic and political infra-structure was. Inadequate roads, sparse government services, and weak political standing contributed to the famine conditions and also made it difficult to get effective assistance to those in need. And the same obstacles stand in the way of helping peasant farmers reassemble the conditions to return to peasant farming. They raise hard issues about when to try to reconstruct the conditions of peasant farming in a devastated region and when to promote resettlement.

The experience of disaster yields lessons about how to prevent similar degradation elsewhere. Experiment stations have devised and tested ways of retaining soil and moisture in dry zones. Strip farming, intercropping, minimum tillage, new crops, reforestation; there is a growing stock of potentially useful policies and techniques to draw upon in protecting against serious environmental damage. In most of rural Africa environmental damage is not an immediate issue or it is still reversible. There is still time to learn how to improve agriculture without putting the environment at risk, but learning takes time, money, and attention. Many think the current effort is much too small and that time is rapidly running out.

Government and market institutions that work

Where the environment is still friendly to peasant farmers but governments and markets fail to respond to their needs and interests, another kind of breakdown occurs. In Ghana with the collapse of cocoa marketing and Uganda in regions not under direct military attack but affected by the collapse of the wage and market economy, peasant farmers increased their reliance on self-provision-ing by shifting resources to food-crop production, resurrecting old crafts to manufacture household goods, and making greater use of hunting and gathering. In Zaire, as well, in regions where government authority became intermittent and arbitrary and roads and markets disintegrated, peasant farmers had to turn to self-provisioning, local trade, and parallel markets to survive. In all three countries peasant-farming communities worked to construct substitute markets and transportation routes, perhaps crossing international borders to link up with better functioning economies. The underground economy of peasant farmers typically has connections with the official political economy, often in the form of payoffs against enforcement or informing. The peasant-farming economy can hardly thrive under conditions of government breakdown; it is weakened and it is not subject to government regulation, but it continues to exist albeit in a constricted form.

The range of levels of survival of peasant farming under duress is very wide. Bare physical and cultural survival is a kind of success under conditions of terrible neglect and difficult environment. In other cases villages and regions have prospered in a kind of enforced self-reliance, as in parts of Ghana's forest zone where cocoa farming had always been restricted precisely by a desire for self-reliance. Where governments have broken down, the task of rebuilding rudimentary authority and reconstructing basic marketing channels is an urgent priority. In most places those institutions function. They may need reform and re-energizing, but they do not need to be built from the ground up.

There are many lessons to draw from this overview of crises, but the one I want to stress here has to do with the surrounding political and economic conditions upon which peasant farming in Africa depends. Where security, climate, or institutional support have broken down, peasant farming is sorely at risk. These three conditions, then, are the minimum requirements for the survival of peasant farming. Where these conditions are met, however, as noted in chapter 1, peasant farming is often failing to expand productivity. Are there any lessons to be drawn from the overview presented here?

THE CHALLENGE

The material challenge in Africa in its starkest terms is to meet human needs and to halt the building crisis of basic production. Hidden in the material challenge is an intellectual one: to grasp the dynamic of social and economic change that is producing the crisis. This book has attempted to clarify the dynamic of change as it affects one important category of Africa's people, the peasant farmers. It started with a critique of the inadequate images of the crisis in Africa (chapter 2), described the nature of peasant farming (chapter 3) and the formation of peasant farming zones (chapter 4), discussed the place of market relations in peasant farming (chapter 5), analysed the stress upon peasant-farming communities (chapter 6), and discussed the wider political dynamics in which peasant farmers have participated as activists and as objects (chapters 7 and 8). A point which the book has reiterated in many ways and in different contexts has been the need for an inclusive perspective on change in peasant-farming communities and in Africa generally.

A broad political economy

At the centre of the analysis are economics and politics, but they immediately imply and involve beliefs and symbols: hence culture and ideology also belong to the core of the study. In farming the interaction with the physical environment is vital to the survival and reproduction of individuals, families, and communities. Considering the impact of pricing policy and of failures of military security, the wider social environment of peasant farming is a vital part of the picture.

We have shown the vital interaction of peasant farming with an environment that is often unstable and intolerant. Although a variety of innovations in tools and crop varieties will certainly help increase the productivity of Africa's peasant farmers, there is no prospect of a massive technological fix for the sector. It follows that the knowledge and skills of the peasant farmers themselves have to be counted as major resources upon which improvements must be built. There is a further implication: the social relations, cultural commitments, and internal social dynamics of peasant farming societies have to be accepted as the starting points for change. The ambition of a broad political economy of peasant farming is to construct a method for grasping the overall social–economic dynamic of any particular peasant-farming region in a way that is relevant to the problems of survival and expansion which the region faces.

At the centre of that dynamic are peasant farmers and peasant-farming communities striving to preserve themselves. The peasant farming units seek to maintain a kind of internal equilibrium which shifts and adapts to changing circumstances. In pursuing that task they adjust their participation in three related circuits of production: production for own consumption; production for sale; and off-farm work for wages or other benefits. Each circuit depends upon fruitful interaction with nature. The agricultural circuits require suitable soil, timely and sufficient rainfall or irrigation water, adequate tools, and necessary seeds. The circuits of production for sale and of wage labour exchange put peasant farmers into wider social networks and transportation systems which depend upon community institutions and also upon government for their security and management. The decisions of peasant-farming units about how to maintain their balance are linked to the working of community institutions and to decisions of governments about how they will support the marketing, labour exchange, and transportation networks vital to peasant farming. Government, on its side, is motivated in part by its interest in the revenue it can gain by taxing agricultural exports and in part by conflicting and shifting interests in regional, class, and individual advantages of both symbolic and material kinds.

In economic terms the crisis of peasant farming in Africa is a crisis of accumulation. It has qualitative as well as quantitative aspects. Accumulation means assigning social and economic resources to improving the production process. In peasant-farming it means increasing and shaping the capacity of the peasant-farming productive machine to make it produce more goods or more valuable goods with the same commitment of labour. In its quantitative aspect, accumulation in peasant farming means more hoes, more machetes, more roads, more cleared land, more producing of tree crops, more marketing points. In its qualitative aspect, it means changing from hoes to oxploughs and tractors, using improved seeds, planting in better ways such as alternating strips of trees and crops, using fertilizer or cattle manure, and protecting land against erosion. A successful programme of accumulation involves all the institutions of peasant-farming: the peasant-farming units; the local community; the government; and the marketing, transporting and supplying institutions. It affects social relations within communities as some farmers expand more rapidly than others and as different farmers choose or are forced into heavier reliance on one or another circuit of production. Market farmers, self-provisioning peasant farmers, and wage-working peasant farmers have different economic interests which sometimes will bring them into conflict. The first question is how, under African conditions, a combined programme of productive accumulation can be achieved. The second question is how the social tensions and conflicts it stimulates can be handled.

With respect to the first question, an understanding of the political economy of peasant farming makes apparent some requirements of a strategy for strengthening production in the sector. First, an adequate strategy needs to develop scientific and applied technical knowledge about ways to improve productivity which fit together with the skills, knowledge, and work pattern of peasant farmers. With few exceptions knowledge relevant to other social and physical environments does not work in Africa without special adaptation, although scattered examples of promising production methods already exist. The right research requires government coordination and international support. Second, a programme for peasant farming has to target community, regional, national, and (ideally) international institutions as well as peasant-farming units. In particular, markets or exchanges which purchase and remove the crop and which supply consumer goods and farming inputs have to give incentive and support to the farming operations. Again, government must at least set the framework for private institutions to work properly. The third necessity of a peasant farming strategy is the political means to handle the social and political conflict which change will generate.

The second question was stressed in chapter 8. Accumulation alters social power as well as economic productivity. The classes, groups, and individuals who decide the way in which the resources will be used to shape production are deciding for the society as a whole, and their decisions affect many kinds of social relations in peasant farming. Changing production in peasant farming is changing a way of life. Therefore much more than economic interests are engaged. There are issues of social prestige and standing among men and women, youth and adults, aristocrats and commoners, and ethnic group and ethnic group. The question of a programme of improving peasant farming must face political and cultural issues as well as economic ones.

There is reason for pessimism about the ability of many governments in Africa to come to grips with the crisis of peasant farming. Does not an adequate policy require exactly the kind of development-oriented state which has yet to appear in Africa? Instead urban bias, personalist politics, administrative incompetence, and inappropriate international assistance stand in the way of effective government action, while volatile and generally worsening prices for export commodities and a rapidly growing population undermine otherwise effective policies.

Some argue that peasant farmers simply have to convert to industrial wage work or capitalist farming by the slow but inevitable turn of the wheel of history. As a type of production they will be crushed, but the smarter and luckier will convert and survive. The trouble with this perspective is that the economic prospects for Africa do not include rapid and broad-based industrialization for many years. Nor will irrigation and a green revolution bring a rapid rural transformation even on the inadequate scale experienced in Asia. Africa's wheel of history seems to pull peasant farming with it, continuing well into the next century and beyond.

Political coalitions
Other patterns, however, are not out of the question. The last chapter noted the pressure on governments from the IMF and the World Bank to improve prices and

research for the more productive and responsive peasant farmers. In political–economic terms we can see this as a proposal for an African-style triple alliance of international finance capital, market-responsive agricultural producers, and national marketing and transporting organizations (private, public, or mixed). Such an alliance would improve research on export crops and food crops that would save foreign exchange. It would promote the most promising peasant farmers and the most promising agricultural crops, favouring larger, more capitalist farmers and advantaged farming zones. The overall policy is one of agricultural export-led growth aimed at maintaining debt payment and international trade. Politically, the dominant coalition would have to rely on a combination of social power, political repression, and political manipulation to keep itself afloat. It would require the state as a fourth member of the alliance. The most fitting ruling ideology for such a coalition is one which attributes to the market the power to exclude peripheral regions and weaker producers. They will be left to keep what balance they can as peasant farmers or rural workers. For Kenya and Côte d'Ivoire such a pattern is conceivable, if the argument that the interests of the larger and more commercial peasant farmers are already well represented in their governing coalitions is correct. Agricultural growth would continue at the price of sharpening and deepening inequality. Smaller farmers and less favoured regions are already paying the price of relative poverty, neglect, and powerlessness.

In countries where the peasant farmers, for whatever reasons, have been more passive as citizens and as producers, a different pattern of peasant farming may be expanded. It is a variant of the state peasantry mentioned in chapter 4. Governments with some unity and ambition may undertake to create more productive peasantries or

managed agricultural schemes. Both socialist and capitalist (or state capitalist) variants of the strategy are possible.
By controlling agricultural projects from above the
government can hope to maximize accumulation on the
basis of highly productive technology. It can also hope to
channel the product into the economy in the manner most
effective for economic growth and to create political
clients over which it has leverage. The only trouble with
this model is that centralized schemes have a miserable
record of performance in Africa. It is difficult to attract, to
train, and to control a population of tenants or workers.
The recent tendency is to move to more decentralized
control over government projects and to use some form of
contract farming or market system. Even were the schemes
to operate effectively, they have severe limitations. They
single out a relatively narrow portion of the rural population for special treatment and leave the others in the same
difficulty they would otherwise encounter. At best the
government will find its balance of payments problem
manageable. At worst it will get the worst of both worlds:
a state-peasant sector that devours investment and gives
little return, and a large and neglected peasant farming
sector unable to improve productivity.

What would a more egalitarian policy of promoting
capitalist peasant farming look like? It would seek to draw
all sizes and regions of peasant farmers into the ruling
coalition and to establish conditions generally favourable
to expansion. In places where larger farmers could hope to
break through to major gains in productivity, they would
not be blocked, but the smaller farmers and more peripheral regions would have a political voice to defend their
interests. The export market and the internal market for
food and industrial goods would begin to dictate winners
and losers among crops and regions. Only with a very
strongly seated ideology of market virtues could the

government handle the political kickback from a market driven strategy. And the government, with international assistance, would need to make research and infrastructure investments and selections.

Socialist governments, as noted in chapter 5, have not found it easy to encompass peasant farming. They might do so if they could limit the degree to which agricultural accumulation created a dominant rural social class. A ceiling could be set on the amount of land or labour one person could manage. In order to minimize the class control which comes from economic inequality, they could also have an explicit policy of developing community services and promoting local democratic practices. Local cooperatives would manage some services and collective investments, but only rarely would farming itself be collectivized. A strong national ideology of socialism and democracy, and a strong national political coalition would be needed to prevent allocational conflicts and conflicting ideas of development from getting out of hand. The policy on peasant farming would be integrated into a wider policy of basic industrialization and increasing self-sufficiency in food and fibre production. The complementarity of interests in the different sectors would be stressed.

A fifth model, unfortunately, will remain part of the picture for some time. Disasters brought on by insecurity, environmental degradation and climate will threaten regions of one or another country in Africa in most years. A system of international assistance ready to go into action needs to be in place, and governments need to see it as part of their work to monitor regions which are at risk and to call for help in good time. Assistance should go beyond relief to rehabilitation and development of stricken peasant-farming regions. The international response to the famine in Ethiopia in 1988 was much more rapid and effective than the response to the 1984 famine, a sign of progress on this front.

Probably in most countries of Africa the real pattern of policy will mix elements from the five models. One thing that is certain is that peasant farming will for a long time be a major economic activity in sub-Saharan Africa. All political and economic strategies need to take more explicit account of peasant farming. A good starting point under all political conditions is to find ways of giving peasant farmers a larger voice in national politics and better forms of organization. There is an opportunity here for peasant farmers to discover their common interests across regional and crop divisions and for incipient class divisions to be faced. A more open politics on peasant farming will broaden the knowledge and the commitments of peasant farmers and of the political coalitions that make policy about them. Several countries in Africa have the political strength to attempt such an opening.

Senegal and Tanzania are examples of the politically more successful governments in Africa. Countries like them could take the initiative in enlarging the practices of local democracy in peasant farming regions and in augmenting an autonomous peasant farmer voice in national politics. There are other examples of relatively successful creation of national political networks, methods of handling conflicts, and ways of compromising distinct interests. In all of them, even the most democratic, the tendency was strong to shift power away from the rural sector, including most peasant farmers, once the necessity of appealing for rural votes was laid to rest. Since the period of electoral politics was relatively short and since it coincided with the peak of the world commodity markets, few governments had to deal with their rural populations at a point where the governments were electorally vulnerable and the peasant farmers had desperate economic and political grievances. It may be time for the stronger governments to face those grievances in a more open politics. The prospect is not an easy one, since government employees, importers, workers, and larger farmers who have drawn advantage from the existing pattern will have to pay the price of change.

The governments whose rural policies and rural sectors are in disarray because of invasion and destabilization have different priorities. Reestablishing security must be the first objective. In the longer run the economic and political reintegration of all the peasant farming regions, taking into account the need for marketing and labour movement, will need to be planned.

Other governments rest on a coalition of forces that is probably incapable of making a significant alliance with rural classes. Traditions and structures of manipulation, exploitation, and neglect are so entrenched that it is difficult to imagine any substantial change without an equally substantial political transition. The realistic potential for programmes to strengthen peasant farming varies greatly from country to country. The kinds of policy which are likely, and which are likely to work, are different under different political and economic conditions. A better understanding of peasant farming will help to see which policies are possible and likely and what their effects might be.

Those peasant farmers who grow export crops are directly linked to world markets. Those who grow crops for domestic markets can help their economies reduce spending on imported food and fibre. The international role of peasant farmers is highly visible in current negotiations of African governments with the IMF, the World Bank, and various consortia of private and governmental lenders. At stake are debt repayment schedules and economic policies. African governments and peasant farmers would benefit enormously from stable prices and consistent markets for the export crops they produce. Price instability and worsening terms of trade have been major causes of economic, social, and political stress in peasant-farming communities in Africa. The policies currently being promoted by the international lenders will tie peasant farming even more tightly to unpredictably fluctuating markets. The instability will accentuate tensions between peasant farmers and their governments and increase stress within peasant-farming communities as different peasant-farming strata are buffeted in different ways by the economic winds. A triple alliance contracted under given price conditions and uniting certain farming regions with government and international capital has limited appeal at the outset, since prices for cotton, oilseeds, coffee, and tea bear very different relations to African costs of production. The alliance will look much different if key prices drop, and the three interests united at one phase may well be at odds at a later stage. The African triple alliance appears to be a recipe for political difficulty.

Unless international agreements stabilize agricultural commodity markets, African governments may be driven to mimic the policies of peasant farmers themselves: to stress self-provisioning in basic agricultural products. A firm decision to move in that direction would give governments a strong and salutary incentive to gain a more complete grasp of the needs and potentials of peasant farmers and to give them a larger voice in the give and take of making policy. It cannot remove all the causes of uncertainty and fluctuation in the markets peasant farmers face, but it can lay the basis for a more respectful and productive politics.

REFERENCES

Af... News. 1987. Vol. 28, No. 5, 16 November.

Ali, T. and J. O'Brien, 1984. 'Labour, Community, and Protest in Sudanese Agriculture'. In J. Barker, ed., *The Politics of Agriculture in Tropical Africa*, pp. 205–238. Beverley Hills: Sage.

Amin, S. 1967. *Le Développement du Capitalisme en Côte d'Ivoire.* Paris: Editions de Minuit.

   ed. 1974. *Modern Migrations in Western Africa.* London: Oxford University Press.

   1976. *Unequal Development: An Essay on the Social Formations of Peripheral Capitalism.* New York: Monthly Review Press.

Apter, D. 1965. *The Politics of Modernization.* Chicago: University of Chicago Press.

Astrow, A. 1983. *Zimbabwe: A Revolution That Lost Its Way?* London: Zed Press.

Awiti, A. 1975. 'Ismani and the Rise of Capitalism'. In L. Cliffe, *et al.*, eds., *Rural Cooperation in Tanzania*, pp. 51–78. Dar es Salaam: Tanzania Publishing House.

Barker, J. 1987. 'Political Space and the Quality of Participation in Rural Africa', *Canadian Journal of African Studies*, Vol. 21, No. 1, pp. 1–16.

Barnett, T. 1977. *The Gezira Scheme: An Illusion of Development.* London: Frank Cass.

Bates, R. 1981. *Markets and States in Tropical Africa.* Berkeley: University of California Press.

Beckford, G. 1972. *Persistent Poverty: Underdevelopment in the Plantation Economies of the Third World.* New York: Oxford University Press.

Beckman, B. 1976. *Organizing the Farmers: Cocoa Politics and National Development in Ghana*. Uppsala: Scandanavian Institute of African Studies.

1981. 'Ghana, 1951–78: The Agrarian Basis of the Post-Colonial State'. In J. Heyer, P. Roberts, and G. Williams, eds., *Rural Development in Tropical Africa*, pp. 143–167. New York: St Martin's Press.

Beer, C. and G. Williams. 1974. 'The Politics of the Ibadan Peasantry', *African Review*, Vol. 4, No. 4.

Bernstein, H. 1979. 'African Peasantries: A Theoretical Framework', *Journal of Peasant Studies*, Vol. 6, No. 4, pp. 421–443.

Bowen, M. 1986. ' "Let's Build Agricultural Producer Cooperatives": Socialist Agricultural Development Strategy in Mozambique, 1975–1983'. Ph.D. dissertation, University of Toronto.

Bryson, J. 1981. 'Women and Agriculture in sub-Saharan Africa: Implications for Development', *Journal of Development Studies*, Vol. 17, No. 3.

Bunker, S. 1987. *Peasants Against the State: The Politics of Market Control in Bugisu, Uganda, 1900–1983*. Urbana: University of Illinois Press.

Burawoy, M. 1985. *The Politics of Production*. London: Verso.

Cabral, A. 1979. *Unity and Struggle*. New York: Monthly Review Press.

Cammack, D. 1987. 'Mozambique: The "Human Face" of Destabilization'. *Review of African Political Economy*, No. 40, December, pp. 65–75.

Campbell, B. 1974. 'Social Change and Class Formation in a French West African State', *Canadian Journal of African Studies*, Vol. 8, No. 2, pp. 285–306.

1978. 'The Ivory Coast'. In J. Dunn, ed., *West African States: Failures and Promises*, pp. 66–116. Cambridge: Cambridge University Press.

Caswell, N. 1984. 'Autopsie de l'ONCAD', *Politique Africaine*, No. 14, June, pp. 39–73.

Chazan, N. 1986. *An Anatomy of Ghanian Politics: Managing Political Recession, 1969–1982*. Boulder: Westview.

Copans, J. 1980. *Les Marabouts de l'Arachide*. Paris: Le Sycomore.

Coquery-Vidrovitch, C. 1969. 'Recherches sur un Mode de Production Africain', *La Pensée*, No. 144, pp. 61–78.

Coulson, A. 1982. *Tanzania: A Political Economy*. Oxford: Oxford University Press.

Cruise O'Brien, D. 1971. *The Mourides of Senegal: The Political and Economic Organization of an Islamic Brotherhood*. London: Oxford University Press.

1979. 'Ruling Class and Peasantry in Senegal, 1960–1976: The Politics of a Monocrop Economy'. In R. Cruise O'Brien, ed. *The Political Economy of Underdevelopment*, pp. 126–155. Beverley Hills: Sage.

David, P. 1980. *Les Navétanes: Histoire des Migrants Saisonniers de L'Arachide en Sénégambie des Origines à Nos Jours*. Dakar: Les Nouvelles Editions Africaines.

Davidson, B. 1969. *The Liberation of Guiné*. Harmondsworth: Penguin.

1976. 'The Politics of Armed Struggle: National Liberation in the African Colonies of Portugal'. In B. Davidson, J. Slovo, and R. Wilkinson, *Southern Africa: The New Politics of Revolution*. Harmondsworth: Penguin.

Demunter, P. 1975. *Luttes Politiques au Zaïre*. Paris: Editions Anthropos.

Dinham, B. and C. Hines. 1983. *Agribusiness in Africa*. London: Earth Resources Research.

Dunmoye, R. 1986. 'The State and the Peasantry: The Politics of Integrated Rural Development Projects in Nigeria'. Ph.D. dissertation, University of Toronto.

Eicher, C. and D. Baker. 1982. *Research on Agricultural Development in sub-Saharan Africa: A Critical Survey'*. Michigan State University International Development Paper No. 1. East Lansing, Michigan: Department of Agricultural Economics, Michigan State University.

Election Study Committee. 1974. *Socialism and Participation: The 1970 Election in Tanzania*. Dar es Salaam: Tanzania Publishing House.

Elmekki, A. 1985. 'Peasants and Capital: The Political Economy of Oilseeds Marketing in the Sudan'. Ph.D. dissertation, University of Toronto.

Esman, M. and N. Uphoff. 1984. *Local Organization*. Ithaca: Cornell University Press.

Fanon, F. 1963. *The Wretched of the Earth*. New York: Grove Press.

Fauré, Y.-A. and Médard, J.-F., eds. 1982. *Etat et Bourgeoisie en Côte d'Ivoire*. Paris: Kathala.

Feldman, R. 1971. *Custom and Capitalism: A Study of Land Tenure in Ismani, Tanzania.* Paper 71.14. Dar es Salaam: Economic Research Bureau, University of Dar es Salaam.

Fortes, M. and E. Evans-Pritchard, eds. 1940. *African Political Systems.* London: Oxford University Press.

Foster-Carter, A. 1978. 'The Modes of Production Controversy', *The New Left Review*, No. 104, pp. 47–77.

Franke, R. and B. Chasin. 1980. *Seeds of Famine, Ecological Destruction and the Development Dilemma in the West African Sahel.* Montclair, New Jersey: Allanheld, Osmun.

Friedmann, H. 1980. 'Household Production and the National Economy: Concepts for the Analysis of Agrarian Formations', *Journal of Peasant Studies*, vol. 1, no. 4, July.

Genoud, R. 1969. *Nationalism and Economic Development in Ghana.* New York: Praeger.

Gervais, M. 1984. 'Peasants and Capital in Upper Volta'. In J. Barker, ed., *The Politics of Agriculture in Tropical Africa*, pp. 127–141. Beverley Hills: Sage.

Geschiere, P. 1982. *Village Communities and the State.* London: Kegan Paul International.

Grier, B. 1987. 'Contradiction, Crisis, and Class Conflict: The State and Capitalist Development in Ghana Prior to 1948'. In I. Markovitz, ed., *Studies in Power and Class in Africa*, pp. 27–49. New York: Oxford University Press.

Halfani, M. and J. Barker. 1984. 'Agribusiness and Agrarian Change'. In J. Barker, ed., *The Politics of Agriculture in Tropical Africa*, pp. 35–64. Beverley Hills: Sage.

Hansen, E. 1987. 'The State and Popular Struggles in Ghana'. In Anyang' Nyongo, ed., *Popular Struggles for Democracy in Africa*, pp. 170–208. London: UNU/Zed Press.

Hansen, M. and M. Marcussen. 1982. 'Contract Farming and the Peasantry: Cases from Western Kenya', *Review of African Political Economy*, No. 23, January–April, pp. 9–36.

Harrison, Paul. 1987. *The Greening of Africa.* London: Paladin.

Helleiner, G. 1966. *Peasant Agriculture, Government, and Economic Growth in Nigeria.* Homewood, Illinois: Irwin.

Heyer, J. 1981. 'Agricultural Development Policy in Kenya from the Colonial Period to 1975'. In J. Heyer, P. Roberts, and G. Williams, eds., *Rural Development in Tropical Africa*, pp. 90–120. New York: St Martin's Press.

Hill, F. 1977. 'Experiments with a Public Sector Peasantry', *African Studies Review*, Vol. 20, No. 3, pp. 25–41.

Hill, P. 1963. *The Migrant Cocoa Farmers of Southern Ghana: A Study in Rural Capitalism*. Cambridge: Cambridge University Press.

   1972. *Rural Hausa, a Village and a Setting*. Cambridge: Cambridge University Press.

   1977. *Population, Prosperity and Poverty: Rural Kano, 1900 and 1970*. Cambridge: Cambridge University Press.

Holmquist, F. 1984, 'Self-Help: The State and Peasant Leverage in Kenya', *Africa*, Vol. 54, No. 3, pp. 72–91.

Hopkins, A. 1973. *An Economic History of West Africa*. London: Longman.

Huddleston, B. 1984. *Closing the Cereals Gap with Trade and Food Aid*. Research Report 43. Washington D.C.: International Food Policy Research Center.

Hyden, G. 1980. *Beyond Ujamaa in Tanzania: Underdevelopment and an Uncaptured Peasantry*. London: Heinemann.

Iliffe, J. 1969. *Tanganyika Under German Rule, 1905–1912*. London: Cambridge University Press.

   1983. *The Emergence of African Capitalism*. Minneapolis: University of Minnesota Press.

Isaacman, A. and B. Isaacman. 1983. *Mozambique: From Colonialism to Revolution, 1900–1982*. Boulder: Westview.

Jackson, R. and C. Rosberg. 1982. *Personal Rule in Black Africa*. Los Angeles: University of California Press.

Jespersen, C. *et al.* 1971. 'Southern Highlands Socio-Economic Survey, Final Report'. Unpublished manuscript, Mbeya, Tanzania.

Jewsiewicki, J. 1980. 'African Peasants and the Totalitarian Colonial Society of the Belgian Congo'. In M. A. Klein, ed., *Peasants in Africa: Historical and Contemporary Perspectives*, pp. 45–75. Beverley Hills: Sage.

Klein, M. 1968. *Islam and Imperialism in Senegal: Sine-Saloum 1847–1914*. Stanford, California: Stanford University Press.

Knight, C. 1974. *Ecology and Change: Rural Modernization in an African Community*. New York: Academic Press.

Leftwich, A. 1983. *Redefining Politics: People, Resources, Power.* London: Methuen.

Lele, U. 1975. *The Design of Rural Development: Lessons from Africa.* Baltimore: Johns Hopkins University Press.

Leo, C. 1984. *Land and Class in Kenya.* Toronto: University of Toronto Press.

Lericollais, A. 1972. *Sob: Etude Géographique d'un Terroir Sérér (Sénégal).* Atlas des Structures Agraires au Sud du Sahara No. 7. Paris: Mouton.

Levi, J. and M. Havinden. 1982. *The Economics of African Agriculture.* Harlow, Essex: Longman.

Lofchie, M. 1986. 'The Decline of African Agriculture: An Internalist Perspective'. In M. Glantz, ed., *Drought and Hunger in Africa,* pp. 85–109. London: Cambridge University Press.

　　1989. *The Policy Factor: Agricultural Performance in Kenya and Tanzania.* Boulder, Colorado: Lynne Rienner.

Machel, S. 1976. *Establishing People's Power to Serve the Masses.* Toronto: Toronto Committee for the Liberation of Southern Africa.

Mafeje, A. 1971. 'The ideology of "tribalism"', *Journal of Modern African Studies,* Vol. 9, No. 2.

Maguire, A. 1969. *Toward 'Uhuru' in Tanzania: The Politics of Participation.* London: Cambridge University Press.

Mair, L. 1962. *Primitive Government.* Baltimore: Penguin.

Mann, J. 1987. 'AIDS in Africa', *New Scientist,* No. 1553, 26 March, pp. 40–43.

Mapolu, H. 1986. 'The State and the Peasantry'. In Shivji, I., ed., *The State and the Working People in Tanzania,* pp. 107–137. Dakar: CODESRIA.

Marx, K. 1963. *The Eighteenth Brumaire of Louis Bonaparte.* New York: International Publishers.

Meillassoux, C. 1977. *Femmes, Greniers et Capitaux.* Paris: Maspero.

Mellor, J., Delgado, and Blackie, eds. 1987. *Accelerating Food Production in Sub-Saharan Africa.* Baltimore: Johns Hopkins University Press.

Mkandawire, T. 1987. 'The State and Agriculture in Africa; Introductory Remarks'. In T. Mkandawire and N. Bourenane, eds. *The State and Agriculture in Africa,* pp. 1–25. London: CODESRIA.

Momba, J. 1982. 'The State, Peasant Differentiation and Rural Class Formation in Zambia: A Case Study of Mazabuka and Monze Districts'. Ph.D. dissertation, University of Toronto.

Morgenthau, R. 1964. *Political Parties in French-Speaking West Africa.* London: Oxford University Press.

Moris, J. 1974. 'The Voter Level Surveys'. In Election Study Committee of University of Dar es Salaam, *Socialism and Participation: Tanzania's 1970 National Elections*, pp. 312–364. Dar es Salaam: Tanzania Publishing House.

Mushi, S. 1971. 'Ujamaa: Modernization by Traditionalization', *Taamuli* (Dar es Salaam) vol. 1, no. 2, March, pp. 13–29.

Mwansasu, B. 1979. 'The Changing Role of the Tanganyika African National Union.' In B. Mwansasu and C. Pratt, eds. *Towards Socialism in Tanzania*, pp. 169–192. Toronto: University of Toronto Press.

Netting, R., D. Cleveland, and F. Stier. 1980. 'The Conditions of Agricultural Intensification in the West African Savannah'. In S. Reyna, ed., *Sahelian Social Development*, pp. 187–506. Abidjan: Regional Economic Development Services Office, West Africa, USAID.

New Scientist 1988. 'Aids Monitor'. In *New Scientist*, No. 1604, 17 March, pp. 30–31.

Pélissier, P. 1966. *Les Paysans du Sénégal: Les Civilisations Agraires du Cayor à la Casamance.* Saint-Yrieix (Haute-Vienne): Imprimerie Fabrègue.

Pipping, K. 1976. *Land Holding in the Usangu Plain. A Survey of Two Villages in the Southern Highlands of Tanzania.* Uppsala: The Scandanavian Institute of African Studies.

Pratt, C. 1976. *The Critical Phase in Tanzania, 1945–1968: Nyerere and the Emergence of a Socialist Strategy.* Cambridge: Cambridge University Press.

Raikes, P. 1975. 'Wheat and Ujamaa Villages'. In L. Cliffe *et al.*, eds., *Rural Cooperation in Tanzania*, pp. 455–479. Dar es Salaam: Tanzania Publishing House.

Ray, D. 1979. 'Administering Rural Development: The Role of Settlement Schemes in Zambia'. Ph.D. dissertation, University of Toronto.

Rey, P.-P. 1973. *Les Alliances de Classes.* Paris: Maspero.

Roesch, O. 1988. 'Rural Mozambique Since the FRELIMO Fourth Congress: The Situation in the Baixo Limpopo'. *Review of African Political Economy*, No. 41, pp. 73–91.

Rothchild, D. and E. Gyimah-Boadi. 1986. 'Ghana's Economic Decline and Development Strategies'. In J. Ravenhill, ed., *Africa in Economic Crisis*, pp. 254–285. New York: Columbia University Press.

Rothchild, D. and V. Olorunsola, eds. 1983. *State Versus Ethnic Claims: African Policy Dilemmas*. Boulder Colorado: Westview.

Sandbrook, R. 1985. *The Politics of Africa's Economic Stagnation*. Cambridge: Cambridge University Press.

Schumacher, E. 1975. *Politics, Bureaucracy, and Rural Development in Senegal*. Berkeley: University of California Press.

Scott, J. 1976. *The Moral Economy of the Peasant: Rebellion and Subsistence in Southeast Asia*. New Haven: Yale University Press.

Stichter, S. 1985. *Migrant Laborers*. Cambridge: Cambridge University Press.

Swindell, K. 1985. *Farm Labour*. Cambridge: Cambridge University Press.

Tabatabai, H. 1986. *Food Crisis and Development Policies in Sub-Saharan Africa*. Geneva: Rural Employment Policy Research Programme, International Labour Office.

Tanzania. 1972. *The Economic Survey 1971–72*. Dar es Salaam: Government Printer.

The Toronto Star. 15 March 1975.

Timberlake, Lloyd. 1985. *Africa in Crisis: The Causes, the Cures of Environmental Bankruptcy*. London: Earthscan, The International Institute for Environment and Development.

Tosh, J. 1980. 'The Cash Crop Revolution in Tropical Africa: An Agricultural Reappraisal', *African Affairs*, Vol. 79, No. 314, January, pp. 79–94.

Van Hekken, P. and H. Van Velsen. 1972. *Land Scarcity and Rural Inequality in Tanzania: Some Case Studies from Rungwe District*. The Hague: Mouton.

Walsh, M. 1985. 'Village, State, and Traditional Authority in Usangu'. In R. Abrahams, ed., *Villagers, Villages, and the State in Modern Tanzania*, pp. 135–167. Cambridge African Monograph 4. Cambridge: Cambridge University Press.

Watts, M. and R. Shenton. 1984. 'State and Agrarian Transformation in

Nigeria'. In J. Barker, ed., *The Politics of Agriculture in Tropical Africa*, pp. 173–204. Beverley Hills: Sage.

Wolpe, H. ed. 1980. *The Articulation of Modes of Production*. London: Routledge and Kegan Paul.

World Bank. 1981. *Accelerated Development in Sub-Saharan Africa: An Agenda for Action*. Washington, D.C.: World Bank.

World Bank. 1984. *Toward Sustained Development in Sub-Saharan Africa*. Washington, D.C.: World Bank.

World Bank. 1986. *Financial Adjustment with Growth in Sub-Saharan Africa*. Washington, D.C.: World Bank.

World Bank. 1987. *World Development Report 1987*. New York: Oxford University Press.

World Bank. 1988. *World Development Report 1988*. New York: Oxford University Press.

Young, S. 1977. 'Fertility and Famine: Women's Agricultural History in Southern Mozambique'. In R. Palmer, and N. Parsons, eds., *The Roots of Rural Poverty in Central and Southern Africa*, pp. 66–81. London: Heinemann.

INDEX

accumulation, economic, 21, 107, 117, 122–123, 202

acquired immune deficiency syndrome (AIDS), 15, 27, 31

African Party for the Independence of Guinea and Cape Verde (PAIGC), 157, 158, 159, 160

Agbekoya rebellion, 23

age-grade association, 147

agricultural extension, 118, 119, 129, 151

agricultural involution, 98

agricultural research, 4, 23, 129, 151

agriculture: annual and perennial crops, 91–93, 122; crisis in, 9, 14–15, 24, 95, 125, 204; economic importance of, 5–8; estate, 158; forest and savanna, 62, 75, 92; importance of, 6, 7, 24; in mineral exporting countries, 7; intensive and extensive, 97; large scale, 90–91; new methods, 114; plantation, 38, 83; positive examples, 14–15, 23; precolonial, 30, 67, 79, 97, 98; self-sufficiency, 12–13; shifting cultivation, 49, 67, 74, 141; see also cash crops; export crops; food crops

AIDS (acquired immune deficiency syndrome), 15, 27, 31

Angola, 7, 19, 28, 82, 125, 156, 158, 159, 160

Ansar, 151

Arusha Declaration, 175

Asante, 132, 174

Baganda, 132

Bagisu, 174

Bamba, Amadu, 147

basic needs: emergency grain supply, 31; purchased necessities, 63; see also cash crops; food; food crops; self-provisioning

BDS (Senegalese Democratic Bloc), 153, 154

beans, 50

Belgian Congo, 18, 147, 153; see also Zaire

Botswana, 7, 179

Burkina Faso (formerly Haute Volta), 19, 95, 179, 182, 189

Burundi, 20

Cabral, Amilcar, 157, 160, 160

Cameroon, 20, 66, 83

capitalist farming, 39 [figure], 40; and productivity, 116–117

cash crops, 17, 21, 50, 62, 82–91; environmental impact, 31, 137–138; and community structure, 84, 85, 88; and family relations, 137–138; and food